BEYOND FEAR AND SILENCE

Beyond Fear and Silence

A Feminist-Literary Approach to the Gospel of Mark

JOAN L. MITCHELL

Continuum
New York London

2001
The Continuum International Publishing Group Inc
370 Lexington Avenue, New York, NY 10017

The Continuum International Publishing Group Ltd
The Tower Building, 11 York Road, London SE1 7NX

Printed in the United States of America

Library of Congress Cataloging-in-Publication Data

Mitchell, Joan L., 1940–
      Beyond fear and silence : a feminist-literary approach to the Gospel of Mark / by Joan
L. Mitchell.
         p. cm.
      Includes bibliographical references and index.
      ISBN 0-8264-1354-4 (pbk.)
      1. Bible. N.T. Mark—Feminist criticism.   I. Title.

   BS2585.2 .M58 2001
   226.3'06'082—dc21
                                                                    2001042203

Contents

Acknowledgments

M ANY PEOPLE HAVE CONTRIBUTED to this book, no one more than Therese Sherlock, who has read and critiqued it in bits, pieces, and chapters and has been part of its becoming from the beginning. She is a gifted, critical reader and a loving and creative friend. As chapter 2 testifies, Elisabeth Schüssler Fiorenza's class on Women in the Gospel awakened feminist reading and purpose for me. At Luther Seminary, Donald Juel's questioning led me to Mark 16:8 as a site for a feminist rereading of Mark. Dr. Juel continued the conversation supportively as my doctoral dissertation advisor.

My mother, Helen Howard Mitchell, inspired me to persist in my studying with her example of going back to school in midlife, driving fifty miles and back every day to summer school, a country school teacher getting a new major. As her daughter, it is no wonder I have found study life-giving and empowering. As the granddaughter of Annie Louise MacFarlane Mitchell, who faithfully kept a one-room branch of the Stearns County Library open in my hometown every Saturday from two to five, it is no wonder I have kept reading.

Helen Coughlan, CSJ, and Eileen O'Hea, CSJ, read the manuscript; their feedback both in the margins and in person buoyed me in finishing the work. My sister Laurel started to read the manuscript in August before she returned to her Head Start classroom. "I think it has important things to tell me," she said, "but I don't know what they are." That was before she got snowed in at Christmas time, finished the manuscript, and said, "I think it's a book."

Numerous people have generously offered places to write. Peter Li invited me to work at his Florida home several different times. I don't know that I could have translated the German I had to read if I couldn't have looked forward to walking the beach each afternoon. Margaret and Bill Hunt opened their Wisconsin home for research, writing, and cross-country skiing. Jeanne Peltier opened her home for final editing and gave the manuscript an encouraging read.

Joan Drury has a special place in this process. Norcroft, her writing residency for women on the north shore of Lake Superior, gave me two life-changing weeks to do nothing but write. Each of the four women writers in residence at Norcroft has a room and a shed. The sheds are four-by-eight, slant-roof buildings that stand in the birch and pine woods surrounding Norcroft lodge. A shed is more than a building. It is an experience of the necessary conditions for writing. A desk spans one long side of each shed. Shelves hold a dictionary and the complete works of the woman authors for whom each shed is named. The desk looks out the window—in my case, onto the lake and its ever-changing colors that light, wind, air, and sun mix each day. A rocker and lots of plug-ins complete the necessities. The Norcroft experience has made me change the structure of my life to include chunks of time for writing and getting whole through hiking or cross-country skiing. I twice took weeks to write at Grand Portage on the north shore. I once took a month at Norcroft alone, where the stars are bright overhead, where at night nothing is lost, none of the women and men in whose loves I've lived—my parents and grandparents; Catherine Kessler and Mary Davida Wood, sisters in the community whose music and mentoring taught me to perform; Mary Kessler, my family (among them the young women I know best); the great scholars whose classes I've taken, whose books I've read, such as Joan and Erik Erikson, who insisted life is intergenerational and epigenetic. As I live in this snowy woods by this great lake without television or other distractions, I have found my mind like the starry sky at night, peppered and peopled with so much love and intellectual light.

This year I lived for a month at Rhys cabin, where Norcrofters can go to continue their work. Again alone, I breathed, awakened daily to the light and sky that are the essentials of the north woods in winter, prayed to be transformed like the trees in falling snow, and rewrote the first half of the book. Its pages hold truth about women I could not walk away from telling.

In readying the book for publication, Frank Oveis has been an editor's editor, wonderfully exact, responsive, and helpful. I have Eileen O'Hea to thank for encouraging me to send the manuscript to him. I also thank Anne H. H. Pyle for her gracious help in procuring the beautiful print of *The Three Women at the Holy Sepulchre* by Japanese artist Sadao Watanabe.

CHAPTER 1

Invitation to Dialogue

❦

1 And when the Sabbath was past, Mary Magdalene, and Mary the mother of James, and Salome brought spices, so that they might go and anoint him. 2 And very early on the first day of the week they went to the tomb when the sun had risen. 3 And they were saying to one another, "Who will roll away the stone for us from the door of the tomb?" 4 And looking up, they saw that the stone was rolled back—it was very large. 5 And entering the tomb, they saw a young man sitting on the right side, dressed in a white robe; and they were amazed. 6 And he said to them, "Do not be amazed; you seek Jesus of Nazareth, who was crucified. He has risen, he is not here; see the place where they laid him. 7 But go, tell his disciples and Peter that he is going before you to Galilee; there you will see him, as he told you." 8 And they went out and fled from the tomb; for trembling and astonishment had come upon them; and they said nothing to anyone, for they were afraid. (Mark 16:1–8)[1]

THIS FINAL SCENE IN THE FIRST WRITTEN GOSPEL resonates with classic descriptions of religious experiences. The hour the evangelist describes in this Easter scene is liminal, the dawning threshold of a new day before light fully discloses fixed line and full color. The place and space are liminal, the open doorway between death and life, between the dark, empty tomb and the world waking to new life. The three women disciples in the narrative experience numinous feelings, those Rudolf Otto identifies as typical of the experience of the holy—terror, awe, fear, fascination.[2] *Trembling* shakes their bones. *Ecstasy* carries them outside themselves and beyond their deepest hopes. *Fear* suspends them in awe and silence, primal religious feelings.

1

By suspending the three women in unspeakable, numinous silence, the Gospel climaxes in an apotheosis, a revelation that has not yet come to words. Once the women speak, this moment of grace and awe will end; words, when they speak them, will describe an experience past rather than present. The narrative preserves the moment and suspends the women deliberately in wordless awe at this threshold.

This book dialogues with the silence of Mary Magdalene, Mary the mother of James and Joses, and Salome in the final verse of Mark's Gospel and with their silencing in the Christian canon and continuing Gospel interpretation. In the earliest and most reliable manuscripts, the first written Gospel ends with Mark 16:8, "They went out and fled from the tomb; for trembling and astonishment had come upon them; and they said nothing to anyone, for they were afraid."[3] No one knows how its original hearers responded to this ending. Rather than accept it as intentional, interpreters theorize that the author never finished writing the Gospel or that the last page of the manuscript got lost.

Today students of the first Gospel usually learn that silence in the form of secrecy is a distinctive literary and theological motif in Mark, what scholars term the "messianic secret."[4] In Mark's narrative Jesus repeatedly tells his disciples and those he heals not to tell who he is. As Jesus leads Peter, James, and John down from the mount where they have seen him in transfigured glory, he insists they tell no one "until after the Son of Man has risen from the dead" (9:9). When the women hear from the young man in the empty tomb that Jesus is risen, the plotted time to broadcast who Jesus is has come. Contrary to this expectation, the narrative suspends the women sent to tell this good news in fear and silence. Why?

This book is a complex answer to this simple question. In fact, the question provokes a rereading of the whole narrative on the literary and feminist premise that these women, their fear and silence, are essential to the story, a necessary part of a literary whole.

The ending of the first Gospel gets negative early reviews. Matthew and Luke find the ending so unsatisfactory that they both rewrite it. Anonymous others generate three alternative endings to the Gospel, including Mark 16:9–20.

In their endings, Matthew and Luke inscribe greater certainty and clear purpose. In Matthew the risen Jesus meets eleven male disciples on a mountain in Galilee, giving them all authority in heaven and on earth and commissioning them to make disciples of all nations (Matt. 28:16–20). In Luke the risen Jesus stands among his confused followers, opens their minds to understand how he fulfills Israel's scriptures, commissions them to be his witnesses, directs them to wait in Jerusalem for the Father's promise, and is carried into heaven near Bethany as they watch (Luke 24:36–53). These endings, in which the risen Jesus himself appears to his male disciples, assures and commissions them, satisfy in a grand and convincing style.

In Luke's Gospel the male disciples dismiss the women's testimony that Jesus has risen as an idle tale (24:11), perhaps addressing nonbelievers' unwillingness to accept the witness of women but nonetheless beginning a process that mutes and minimizes, even if it cannot totally erase, the women's importance.[5] To a feminist reader like me, interpreters seem all too ready to dismiss the women's witness and judge them characters too timid or too gullible to hand on the news of Jesus' resurrection authoritatively. However, feminist scholar Mary Ann Tolbert concludes that in the end the women disciples fail just as the men disciples do when they flee at Jesus' arrest and as Peter does when he denies Jesus.[6] But why, one has to ask, hand on a story of total failure as if somehow later disciples might succeed where those who knew Jesus face to face did not?

In defense of those who have sought to fix and improve Mark's original ending, one must admit that, like comedy, effective rhetoric turns on what an author can depend an audience knows. An audience ten years later or in a new geographic area may no longer know the women were anything but silent about the message in their lifetimes, making the original ending confusing and disappointing rather than a call to believe their now-written witness.

An experience of seeing a 1990s college production of the 1960s musical *Hair*, a play that roused my generation into antiwar protest and sang our hopes for the Age of Aquarius to dawn, demonstrated to me how differently a later generation can react. I attended the 1990s production with a friend my age whose youngest brother was killed in Vietnam; with my youngest sister, who married a Vietnam vet, one of the 40 percent of his company who survived the Tet offensive; and their daughter. A young man named Claude is the main character in *Hair*. He is torn between burning his draft card and enlisting in the army, between his exuberant love of life and his patriotic ideals. When Claude, who "believes in God and believes in Claude," comes on stage for the final scene of the play, he is wearing the military fatigues of a new recruit. Both my friend and I saw the back of his shirt full of bullet holes and blood. Neither my younger sister nor her daughter, ten and thirty years younger, saw the holes. My friend and I understood Claude's act of signing up for the draft as a sentence of death and the final song, "Let the Sun Shine" as a plea for peace and an end to senseless killing. We had belonged to the original audience of *Hair*. My friend had her own brother's death with which to verify Claude's death. My sister and niece, however, saw in Claude's flag-draped body a testimony to patriotism and heard "Let the Sun Shine" as a blessing on his growing up enough to do his duty. "He wasn't dead," they both said.

"Didn't you see his back was full of bullet holes?" I asked.

They hadn't. They were a new audience. They saw the production having spent years trying to appreciate what my brother-in-law had risked for his country in Vietnam. Perhaps like the original audience of *Hair*, Mark's audience had more to fear than the communities for whom Matthew and Luke wrote in the 80s C.E.

This book contends that Mark deliberately characterizes Jesus' first disciples, both men and women, as frequently afraid and amazed beyond words. Hearers of this Gospel have reason for their fear. Jesus, after all, was crucified for claiming to be Israel's messiah. Following Jesus has cost James, Peter, and Paul their lives by the time the Gospel is written around 70 C.E. By characterizing the women in fear and silence, the first Gospel speaks to its audience, understanding fear and uncertainty not as failure but as the existential threshold where faith begins.

This book will make the case that Mark's Gospel values the women's witness. In the first written Gospel, the disciples in history become characters in story, no longer living and breathing but forever frozen in the significance the author wants readers to see in them. In my reading the three awestruck women who flee the tomb conflate with an artist's painting of them on the wall behind the baptismal font in the house church at Dura-Europos.[7] The painting from the mid-third century makes the women midwives of baptismal rebirth. The Gospel paints a similar tableau in words at its end. The three women disciples become forever Easter women, who invite new generations of hearers to profess the faith the young man in the white robe speaks in the tomb. Their role as characters is to invite hearers to step across the threshold of faith, into the death and resurrection of Jesus, the Christ, the one John the Baptist prophesies is coming after him and will baptize with the Holy Spirit (Mark 1:7–8).

My interpretation makes Mark's Easter story (16:1–8) a potentially dangerous memory. What if the research and interpretation in this book prove convincing? What if the women have a distinctive place in tradition at the tomb become womb of faith and at the font in which faith comes to birth? How might the women's reclaimed significance among Jesus' first disciples affect the case two thousand years later of Sister of St. Anne Jeannette Normandin, fired from her ministry and ordered to leave her residence for wearing an alb and stole and assisting at the baptism of two babies—that is, for performing clerical duties?[8] Sister Jeannette served Immaculate Conception Parish in Boston for eleven years, raised money for Ruah House for poor women with AIDS and HIV, and ministered throughout fifty-two years of religious life with women in prison, women who are drug dependent, and women who are mentally ill or dying. We know nothing comparable about Mary Magdalene's life and ministry in the forty years between Jesus' death and resurrection and the writing of the Gospel, though legends take her to France preaching the good news. If Mary Magdalene were Jesus' age, then in 70 C.E. she would have been in her seventies like Sister Jeannette, a woman who had given her life to the Christian community, a pioneering disciple of long-established integrity and wholehearted commitment. What if she were well known in the Christian community for telling the story she doesn't tell in the narrative?

In its final characterization of Mary Magdalene, the first Gospel freezes her in fear and silence. The same narrative suspends Peter in tears and says no more about him (14:72). But Peter's silence and tears don't undercut his leadership the way Mary Magdalene's fear and silence discredit her witness. The canonical tradition begins a silencing of these women that interpreters through the centuries have continued.

A feminist interpreter cannot help but see patriarchal bias in the later Gospels' willingness to silence and minimize the three women as witnesses. In *Women's Ways of Knowing*, the authors describe silence as the negative state of women who have internalized their worthlessness in the eyes of spouse, parents, and society and been paid too little attention to bother putting their experience into words.[9] Why in their subsequent retellings do Matthew and Luke eliminate the women's silence at the end of the first Gospel and downplay the significance of their witness, in effect silencing or discrediting them? A feminist suspects bias and uses suspicion as an interpretive tool to recover women's importance in the Gospels and compensate for the negative tendency in the tradition and its interpretation to minimize, marginalize, trivialize, silence, and erase women's presence among Jesus' disciples.

Once I observed a middle-aged couple argue in sign language at a bus stop. Her fingers raced in vigorous motion close to his face. He shrugged, returned a quick gesture, and turned away. She stepped around in front of him and began signing again in staccato gestures. To this he turned his back and made her invisible to him, the way cats do when they want you to know you have displeased them. The light turned green and I drove on, having glimpsed as invisibility the turning away from dialogue that I, as a hearing person, usually experience as silence.

Dialogue with silence is familiar to women. Men talk more than women because women do the work of responding to the conversations men initiate more often than men respond to the exchanges women initiate.[10] Dialogue with silence is familiar to women in our Roman Catholic community of faith. We can't talk about the ordination of women. Sister Jeanine Grammick can neither continue her ministry with people who are gay and lesbian and their families nor talk about being silenced. If the emergence of women, the recognition of full personhood for half the human race, is the defining characteristic of the twentieth century,[11] women becoming visible and finding voice must appear dangerous and out of place to the men whose role it is to uphold the church's present hierarchical order. How would they learn that their male experience is not generic, that women's experience differs from their own? Some listen but too many temporize, hedge, appreciate us in our place, shrug, and turn away. They put me in mind of my brother when he complains that his young-adult kids talk to their mother and don't listen to him. At these times he sounds like a parent still expecting obedience of grown children, rather than an adult willing to engage with an equal in a mutually transforming exchange.

When Francis Cardinal George of Chicago invited Anice Schervish and two other lay ministry students to meet with him about women's ordination, the women took with them eighty letters from other women "feeling discounted and unwelcome in their communities, their gifts ignored." Cardinal George took time to listen with respect, Ms. Schervish reports.[12] The conversation that follows is her memory of their dialogue, which she regarded as cordial. She expects he will read the letters.

"One's own experience is not and cannot be normative for the church," the cardinal states.

"Those who have been determining the norms for two thousand years have all been celibate males," Anice replies. "You can use your position to be prophetic."

"Prophecy is standing for the truth that is Jesus Christ," says the cardinal.

"We are being prophetic," Anice answers.

"It's not about experience; it's about revelation. Our culture is influencing you. We are not an enlightenment people. We are a people of revelation, which was closed with the death of the last apostle," Cardinal George responds.

This conversation ends with certainty, like the Gospels of Matthew and Luke, not in deliberate ambiguity that invites interpretation, like Mark's empty tomb and the women in speechless awe. Is culture speaking in the women's experiences and not the Spirit of truth, who will guide us into all truth (John 16:13)? This question is key. The ending of Mark's Gospel seems worth reclaiming for its fit with our postmodern culture, which welcomes the voices of women and men, all races, every status, and multicultures into a widening conversation of unfolding truth. The ending of Mark's Gospel invites dialogue with the tradition it hands on. The discourse walks us to the empty tomb, an ambiguous and existential symbol. It is a real grave, a place of death, but empty, a potential space for faith.[13] What does Jesus' real absence from the tomb say? What if we had no other Gospels to assure us the crucified Jesus appeared among his disciples in a new way, vindicated, divinity showing through and transforming his wounded body? What if we had only the story, its testimony, its truth claims—ours to test and let resonate with our experience? This is the threshold the first Gospel creates.

Where a story begins and ends is what writing narrative is all about. Where does the Gospel narrative begin and end? For Matthew, Jesus is the messiah whose genealogy places him in Israel's history as son of David and Abraham. In Luke's orderly account of how Jesus fulfills Israel's scriptures, the evangelist carefully places Jesus' birth in Gentile history when Herod is king in Judea, Augustus emperor in Rome, and Quirinius governor of Syria. In Luke's genealogy Jesus is the son of Adam and God, a savior for all of good will. John's Gospel begins with Wisdom, who pre-exists with God, comes into the world, takes flesh, and dwells among us in Jesus.[14]

For Mark, Jesus' story belongs in the line of Israel's prophets. Jesus' story begins with the voice of the prophet John the Baptist. To the author of Mark, John the Baptist sounds like the earlier prophet Second Isaiah, whose voice cried out in the wilderness to prepare a road for God to come among the people in exile and bring them home (1:2–3). John the Baptist prophesies that one more powerful will come after him who will baptize with the Spirit. Indeed when John baptizes Jesus with water, the heavens are torn open (*schizomenous*) and the Spirit descends upon Jesus, driving him into the desert for forty days. Jesus' ministry in Galilee comes after John is imprisoned. He is a voice announcing, "The kingdom of God has come near. Repent and believe in the good news" (1:14–15). When immediately in the narrative Jesus calls Andrew, Peter, James, and John (1:16–20), he doesn't say, "Follow me," but "Come after me." Mark's Gospel is about a successive line of prophets. By 70 C.E. when Mark's Gospel is written, Jesus' men and women disciples have taken their turn. They have come after Jesus and done their fishing for believers. As characters in Mark's Gospel, they call a new generation to prophetic faith. The author of Mark crafts the narrative and rhetoric of the first written Gospel to call its hearers to come and take their places in the long line of prophets who have given their lives to the good news of God's faithful, life-giving love: Isaiah, John the Baptist, Jesus, Peter, Andrew, James, John, Mary Magdalene, Mary the mother of James and Joses, Salome.

As women have begun to study theology in the last two centuries, women scholars have critiqued scripture, tradition, and theology for their silences about women. How do we receive and transform a tradition biased against us? It is the same question people who aren't white in race or European in culture must ask. How do I receive and liberate a tradition that accepts slavery? How do I receive a tradition to which my culture is invisible and without value? In Mark's Gospel a Syrophoenician woman, a double outsider because she is both foreign and female, teaches the teacher Jesus and shows us how: she speaks the truth of her experience to him when he refuses to help her. She finds her voice. She talks back to the voice of authority that dismisses her. She insists on dialogue (Mark 7:24–30). In the Gospel the woman succeeds in changing Jesus' mind. He enlarges his mission to include her. This story anticipates the need for dialogue between voices of experience and voices of authority in every age if faith is to live.

The first written Gospel gives Jesus' women disciples very little visibility and even less voice. In the two verses that describe women standing at a distance from his cross (15:40–41), Mark reveals that Mary Magdalene, Mary the mother of James and Joses, Salome, and many other women followed and served Jesus and came with him from Galilee. These two verses give us permission to see women disciples with Jesus throughout his ministry from its beginning in Galilee to its end in Jerusalem at the cross, burial, and empty tomb.

Until I took Elisabeth Schüssler Fiorenza's class entitled "Gospel Stories of Women" in 1986, I gave these few verses about the women disciples of Galilee no more significance than tradition or its interpreters. Her classroom praxis gave me my first experience of feminist liberation theology in action. She lectured twice on her books, assigned reading, and refused to conduct a learned monologue. Instead she put us to work in groups where knowledge shared became knowledge transformed. Indeed we all had knowledge and experience out of which to construct thought.

The class included serious academic students like myself, many women ministers from the Boston area who often came pushing a child in a stroller, and Catholic sisters on sabbatical, most of whom had extensive experience doing liberation theology in base communities among the poor in Latin America. The Franciscan sister who sat next to me had been in El Salvador. Unforgettably she recounted gathering with poor women to reflect on the scriptures and agreeing to make a commitment together to act. At this point, a leader took a single stalk of wheat and broke it. Then the leader passed single stalks of wheat to each of the women, and each in turn contributed her stalk to form a bundle that could not be broken. The bundle expressed solidarity far deeper than any political organizing I had experienced around an achievable policy change. The bundle stood for sustained commitment to transforming the systemic evils of poverty, racism, and sexism in which the women lived. Putting their stalks together expressed willingness to do what was needed for one another on the way to greater change. Such was the richness of experience students brought into our conversation. Such is the solidarity women experience in speaking the truth of their lives.

Professor Schüssler Fiorenza gave each group a Gospel story about a woman, her four feminist principles of Bible interpretation, and a bibliography. We were to work together and use these to prepare a presentation on the passage for the whole class. Those who wanted credit had to write out the presentation as a paper. The four principles of feminist interpretation challenged us to:

1. Suspect androcentric and patriarchal biases in the passage.

2. Reconstruct the passage historically with the women at the center rather than at the margin.

3. Consider how to proclaim the passages in our churches.

4. Actualize the women's silences in the text creatively, by using our own voices to let them speak.[15]

This teaching process gave everyone in the class voice. Professor Schüssler Fiorenza led an exhaustive critique of every class presentation.

We learned from each other. We helped each other read what the text said rather than what we had been taught it meant. Some were already accomplished at hearing silences and identifying how generic male-centered language makes women invisible in the story. I had my first experience of liberating feminist praxis in which many participants nourish each other rather than one vocal superior feeding a whole group of silent inferiors. This feminist praxis was not out to claim what men have, to reverse patriarchy as if matriarchy would be a sure-fire improvement. In making room to hear women, this praxis insisted on joining with all others marginalized by race, class, sexual orientation, or poverty in constructing a more just and inclusive community as our life together.

Without the lens of feminist biblical interpretation, I saw in the Gospels Jesus, his twelve male disciples, and crowds of suppliants and curiosity seekers. By moving the women at the tomb from the margin to the center of interpretation, I discovered that silence and fear characterize not only these three women disciples but also the men disciples. Besides suspending Peter broken down in tears after denying Jesus, the narrative leaves Jesus' other disciples fleeing at his arrest. In fact, in the first Gospel silence and fear are the good ground in which faith grows, the threshold of faith.

Tradition remembers the names of Mary Magdalene, Mary the mother of James and Joses, and Salome. The Gospel knows the names of Peter, James, and John, whom with Andrew Jesus calls to "come after" him and fish for people (1:17) and who frequently accompany Jesus and speak in the Gospel. It knows the names of twelve whom Jesus appoints to be with him and to proclaim his message (3:14–19). But never as characters in Mark's narrative do these earliest disciples who know Jesus face to face in history ever tell anyone that Jesus is the messiah. Jesus sends the twelve out two by two (Mark 6:7). They proclaim repentance, cast out many demons, and anoint people with oil, which cures many (6:12–13). The Gospel gives them no speaking parts; they make no claims about who Jesus is on this mission.

Later, in Mark 8:27–30, Jesus asks his disciples who people think he is and who they think he is. Peter speaks for the group and professes, "You are the messiah." After a one-verse warning to tell no one about him, Jesus predicts, for the first of three times, that he will suffer, die, and be raised up. Peter reacts disapprovingly, showing us readers or hearers of the story that he has the right word for who Jesus is but a popular, unexamined notion of its meaning. Many interpreters see Jesus' disciples in Mark's Gospel, both men and women, as a failed and hapless lot. However, examining the women's fear and silence as literary motifs reveals a pattern in Mark's characters, a contrast between these failed disciples and anonymous suppliants who irrepressibly tell the secret the well-known others keep.

Feminist Bible interpretation is a liberation theology, which reads with a preferential interest in those characters whom the main story minimizes, marginalizes, silences. It reads from the bottom of the Gospel's social world up rather than from the top down. At the bottom of this social world are many poor suppliants and seekers who lay claim to Jesus' power. Four of these anonymous people spread the secret that Jesus' closest disciples keep. The four model the Gospel's ideal response to Jesus—personally testifying that Jesus has healed them. Their anonymity helps give them a representative quality. They can become those in need or curious about Jesus in every generation. They testify to the power of faith in Jesus. Interpretation and preaching usually focus on Jesus and see the suppliants as inferior, insignificant characters—little people, minor characters.[16] Feminist interpretation decenters this focus, moving it from Jesus and his male disciples to the women disciples, the women suppliants, and other suppliants, several of whom turn out to be the model believers in the narrative.

Hearers and readers of the word, who like them move from fear to faith, take their places in a long line of God's prophets who give their lives to speaking God's word at whatever cost. They call to every next generation that encounters the Gospel to follow in their time. This book looks with the women in Mark's narrative from a past that included them toward a future in which they have full voice in the company of present-day believers.

At stake in how people today interpret Mark's Gospel is who has voice in our Christian community. Who interprets the Gospel traditions we receive? Who says what the silence of these women invites or disallows? The silence of the three women of Galilee awaits attentive dialogue with women today.

Chapter 2, "History Becomes Story," establishes a literary perspective on Mark's Gospel. It examines the grammar and syntax of Mark 16:8. It observes the author at work in Jesus' trial scene, constructing a threshold of response for the reader like the threshold at the Gospel's end, orienting the narrative forward in time toward its audience. It articulates how the implied author of the Gospel, its omniscient narrator, makes historical eyewitnesses into literary characters whose witness is signatory to the story's truth.

Chapter 3, "Feminist Suspicion," explains suspicion as a feminist principle of interpretation and critiques the interpretations of Mark 16:8 in the Christian canon, tradition, and lectionary. Chapter 4, "Liberating Reading," identifies the feminist, literary, and liberation principles of interpretation this study uses to dialogue with the women's fear and silence in Mark 16:8.

Chapter 5, "Women of Galilee," brings the women at Jesus' cross, burial, and empty tomb from the margin to the center of interpretation, recognizing that women follow, serve, and accompany Jesus from Galilee to Jerusalem, and that his disciples include many women. Chapter 6, "Numinous Fear," finds that the literary motif of fear is key to Mark's theology of discipleship, especially in the scenes the narrative places between the two stories of Jesus crossing and calming the Sea of Galilee (Mark 4:35–6:52). The narrative makes the woman with the hemorrhage the ideal disciple in this section, the one who moves from fear to faith. Chapter 7, "Silence, Secrets, and Speech," explores the theme of the messianic secret in Mark, showing the many ways the implied author constructs silences in the narrative to persuade hearers and readers to voice their faith. Chapter 8, "Calling a New Generation," examines the intergenerational context of the first written Gospel and identifies five time periods at play in the narrative, namely, Israel's prophetic past, the story time of Jesus' ministry (30 C.E.), the mission time of the eyewitness disciples (30–70 C.E.), the writing time of the evangelist (about 70 C.E.), and the time of every audience that receives the Gospel. In this setting the four anonymous suppliants, who tell the secret the named men and women disciples keep, become the model believers for a new generation.

Chapter 9, "Narrative and Reader," analyzes how dialogue between written Gospel and hearers takes the place of face-to-face dialogue between storyteller and audience and creates potential space for dialogue with indeterminate audiences, with us today. Chapter 10, "Emancipatory Dialogue with Tradition," reflects on the Syrophoenician woman of Mark 7:24–30 as a model of how to receive and transform tradition biased against women. In the epilogue Mary Magdalene speaks briefly.

CHAPTER 2

History Becomes Story

⚜

T HE FIRST GOSPEL ENDS in unexpected and unsatisfying silence, which this book interprets as an artfully crafted turn to the audience to create a threshold or potential space for faith. In Mark 16:8, the original final verse of the first Gospel, three women—Mary Magdalene, Mary the mother of James, and Salome—tell no one that they entered Jesus' tomb, found it empty, and heard a young man inside the tomb proclaim, "You seek Jesus of Nazareth, who was crucified. He has risen; he is not here; see the place where they laid him" (16:6). They tell no one that the young man sends them to affirm a prophetic promise, "Go, tell his disciples and Peter that he is going before you to Galilee. There you will see him as he told you" (16:7). The two Marys and Salome flee the tomb, ecstatic and trembling, but say nothing to anyone, because the first Gospel says in its final clause, "they were afraid" (16:8).

Silence and fear are the telling details the author selects to characterize the women at the empty tomb. Authors create an illusion of a whole, real world through the details they select to tell any story. They leave unsaid all but the most necessary and telling details. They don't run their characters through every step of their routines or tell readers everything about a person. The first Gospel does not say the women never tell the good news that Jesus is risen.[1] It simply ends with their fear and silence for a literary effect the author wants.

If we judge by how frequently and complexly the first Gospel explores fear, this feeling must characterize the audience for whom Mark writes. The writing of the first Gospel responds to two coincident happenings— the destruction of the Jerusalem Temple and the deaths or aging of the original eyewitness disciples. In 70 C.E. Christians have to wonder who they are without the Temple, about their staying power without their first charismatic leaders, and about their continuity with Jesus' message without the eyewitnesses.[2] In concluding the first Gospel with the three women's silence, Mark recognizes that dialogue with Jesus' message must in the future take place with this written narrative, because it can no longer take place face to face with eyewitness preachers. They have been martyred for their witness like James and Peter, have died, or have grown very old.

This chapter examines the implied author at work crafting Christian oral tradition into written narrative with an ending that deliberately suspends the first witnesses of Jesus' resurrection in fear and silence. Close examination shows that the syntax of the Gospel's final verse winds down to a deliberate close. The narrative uses silence not only to create a threshold of faith in 16:8 but also to enhance the few revealing words Jesus speaks during his trial. In fact, the author splices Jesus' trial within Peter's denial, orienting the story so only the reader can respond to its deepest level. Mary Magdalene, Mary the mother of James and Joses, Salome, and the other women of Galilee are pivotal characters in the narrative. Their fear and silence in the Gospel's final verse invite hearers of the narrative to respond. Their characterization identifies them with other characters and motifs within the literary narrative. Their role as the omniscient narrator's eyewitnesses of the final and culminating events of Jesus' life links them to history. To the audience the women witnesses function as midwives of faith. In the story world they are disciples suspended at the threshold between fear and faith. As historical figures become story characters, they are the signatory witnesses who testify at the boundary of the text that the narrative is historically true.

SYNTAX

Some interpreters regard Mark's ending as too abrupt to be deliberate. The story must be unfinished or the ending lost. However, the grammar and syntax of Mark 16:8 show a carefully constructed verse in two parallel parts. In v. 8a, the women flee the tomb (an action), for they are trembling and astonished (the feelings that motivate their action). In v. 8b, they say nothing (an inaction), for they are afraid (the feeling that motivates their silence).

> 16:8a   And they went out and fled from the tomb;
>   for trembling and astonishment had come upon them;
>
> 16:8b   and they said nothing to anyone,
>   for they were afraid.

The conjunction "for" in English, *gar* in Greek, links the clauses in both v. 8a and v. 8b. Greek word order always places a conjunction second in a sentence, which makes Mark's Gospel break off in Greek with a conjunction.[3]

> 16:8a   *kai exelthousai ephygon apo tou mnēmeiou;*
>   *eichen gar autas tromos kai ekstasis.*
>
> 16:8b   *kai oudeni ouden eipan,*
>   *ephobounto gar.*

The final *gar* creates an especially abrupt ending to the Gospel. However, the author has artfully shortened the clauses to wind the syntax down toward the *gar*. The two halves of v. 8a each have six words in Greek; the two halves of v. 8b wind down to four words, then two.[4] The Easter narrative that ends the first Gospel breaks off without the women executing their commission to tell Jesus' disciples he goes ahead of them into Galilee (16:7); it breaks off without the male disciples learning in the text that Jesus has been raised up as he promised at the beginning of the passion story in Mark 14:28. Actually, the Gospel breaks off no more abruptly than the first verse of the Gospel breaks into the narrative, "Here begins the good news of Jesus Christ, the Son of God" (1:1).

The women's silence in Mark 16:8b creates a puzzle that makes the reader implicitly ask why.[5] By breaking off, the text leaves the unlocking of the last sentence and the entire Gospel to the reader. As the syntactical rhythm moves from action to cause—from flight to its cause, terror and amazement; from silence to its cause, fear—and as the story ends, the hearer (assuming that texts in the late first century were normally for reading aloud)[6] hears silence and experiences the puzzle. In our own century, when individual, silent Bible reading is more common, the ending brings the reader abruptly out of the story world of the text into his or her own present world. A conjunction dangles as the final perimeter of the story world while ecstasy (*ekstasis*) holds the story characters speechless and beside themselves in the terror and astonishment of a divine revelation.

The Christian who writes Mark's Gospel dares to address hearers with a rhetoric of summons, a dynamic expectation that hearers can and will finish the suspended ending of the story. The writer places the women as midwives at the boundary of the text, ready to help hearers' faith come to birth, expecting them to dialogue with their silence, to interpret the story, and weigh its truth claims. Implicitly, the writer has a midwife's perspective that this new invention, the written Gospel, will assist the birth of faith and discipleship in new generations of hearers who have within them the ability to interpret and respond to story.

DISCOURSE

Discourse is *how* a writer tells a story, its arrangement for effect. Discourse orients a narrative to its audience. Anyone who wants to argue that the three women are silent because that's what really happened in history, not because an author has deliberately constructed an ending for readers' or hearers' response, must reckon with the silence the implied author artfully constructs around Jesus during his trial and passion. Mark uses silence in the plot of the passion narrative as deliberately as he does at the end of the Gospel, orienting it to the audience.

After his last supper with his friends, Jesus prophesies, "You will all become deserters; for it is written, 'I will strike the shepherd, and the sheep will be scattered.' But after I am raised up, I will go before you to Galilee" (14:27–28). Jesus insists that Peter will deny him three times before morning. In his last words as he is arrested, Jesus says, "Let the scriptures be fulfilled" (14:49). In these words he prophesies an inexorable sequence of events and prepares the hearer for all that follows in the narrative. Between these words and his wordless cry as he dies, Jesus says only "I am" (*Egō eimi*), "You say" (*Sy legeis*), and three times alludes to Israel's scriptures. In telling Jesus' passion, the first Gospel deliberately asserts Jesus' messianic identity more prominently on the lips of the false witnesses, chief priests, and Pilate, while Jesus himself says little.

At his trial, Jesus stands silent before the high priest as false witnesses accuse him of saying, "I will destroy this temple that is made with hands, and in three days I will build another, not made with hands" (14:58).[7] His silence frustrates the high priest into asking directly, "Are you the Messiah, the Son of the Blessed One?" Jesus' silence heightens the importance of what he does say, in this case a full confession in two words that he is the messiah. Jesus answers, "I am" (*egō eimi*), then adds prophetically: "you will see the son of Man seated at the right hand of

Power . . . coming with the clouds of heaven" (14:62). *Egō eimi* is the name for God in the Greek Old Testament, the Septuagint; it translates the Hebrew name Yahweh. The prophecy that follows the "ego eimi" echoes Psalm 110, which honors Israel's king with a seat at God's right hand, and Daniel 7:13, which describes one like a human coming on the clouds. Later, when Pilate asks Jesus, "Are you the king of the Jews?" (15:2), Jesus again answers tersely, "You say" (*Sy legeis*), then refuses Pilate's requests to answer the chief priests' many accusations. The passersby and leaders who mock Jesus on the cross repeat the accusations of the false witnesses, "You who would destroy the temple and build it in three days, save yourself, and come down from the cross" (15:29–30). Jesus remains silent until shortly before he dies, when he prays the question that begins Psalm 22, "My God, my God, why have you forsaken me?" Between Jesus' arrest (14:42–50) and his death (15:39), Mark's narrative constructs silence that makes Jesus' anguish, his *egō eimi* statement (I am the messiah), and its supporting allusions resound.

The author orients the trial narrative toward the reader and deliberately composes it to keep Jesus' messianic identity secret from all but the reader.[8] The Gospel is both a story in which its characters participate and a discourse that prestructures readers' response. Seymour Chatman usefully distinguishes between the two levels of narrative. Story refers to the actions and happenings that constitute plot, the characters, and settings; in other words, story is the content of narrative form. Discourse is the expression of narrative form, "the means by which the content is communicated." Story is the *what* in a narrative; discourse is the *how*.[9] By arranging Jesus' trial scene so only the reader or hearer knows who Jesus is, the author of Mark prestructures a response of faith in the audience here as in Mark 16:8.

Another indicator that an author constructs a literary threshold at the end of the Gospel is how artfully the discourse splices Jesus' trial (14:55–65) into Peter's denial (14:53–54 and 66–72). In the narrative Peter follows the arrested Jesus to the high priest's house and takes a seat in the courtyard by the fire to warm himself. With Peter seated outside, the narrative cuts to the trial going on inside the house, where the assembled chief priests, scribes, and elders hear false witnesses fail to agree in their testimony against Jesus. When Jesus answers, "I am," to the high priest's question, "Are you the Messiah, the Son of the Blessed One?" the assembly inside agrees that Jesus has blasphemed and deserves death; some begin spitting on him. Then the narrative cuts back outside to Peter, where the plot left him warming himself by the fire. Servant girls and bystanders begin interrogating him about his relationship to Jesus, a parallel with the questioning of Jesus inside. Peter three times denies that he even knows Jesus. This intercut of Jesus' trial between Peter's following to the courtyard and subsequent denial creates a scene with inside and outside dimensions. In effect, Peter's denial and Jesus' trial happen concurrently. The religious officials condemn Jesus, and one of his closest disciples repudiates him at the same time. However, only the omniscient narrator and the reader know that Peter is denying Jesus outside as Jesus is revealing his identity as the messiah and Son of the Blessed One inside. In setting up the irony, the implied author makes space between inside and outside, between the officials' condemnation and Peter's denial, space for a third response to the scene: the reader or hearer's recognition of Jesus' secret messianic identity.

From the Gospel's first verse both the omniscient narrator and the reader know this story is about Jesus, the messiah, the Son of God. Mark develops a secrecy motif in the narrative that is incomplete without the reader, whose voice can respond to the silence constructed as the ending of the text. None of the first male disciples or the female disciples ever tells the secret of who Jesus is in the story. Mark makes the narrative accessible as its deepest level only to the reader and not to the characters in the story.[10] As literature rather than history, Mark's Gospel refers forward toward its readers and hearers, calling them to faith.

SIGNATORY WITNESSES

The first evangelist tells Jesus' story from the God's-eye view of an omniscient narrator. Every story has a teller; every written narrative, an author who seeks so to mesmerize hearers and readers that the plot and characters become real. An omniscient narrator invisibly oversees the plot and becomes the anonymous voice that hearers forget is telling the story, putting the scenes in order, setting up prophecies that comes true, paralleling characters, deliberately setting up silences and echoes that work like oral road maps through the story. In contemporary writing, most flesh-and-blood authors choose to tell their stories more realistically through one character that is participating in the narrative. This limits the plot to what this character experiences and learns of others' actions and motivation. An omniscient narrator, however, knows all and in Mark's Gospel can report Jesus' interior prayer in the garden, even with all possible eyewitness characters asleep in the scene. In the scenes of Jesus' death, burial, and proclaimed resurrection, the omniscient narrator chooses to have witnesses to verify the narrative.

Mary Magdalene and Mary the mother of James and Joses witness Jesus' death, burial, and resurrection. Salome witnesses Jesus' death and resurrection with them but not his burial. The women disciples' presence in Mark 15:40–41, 15:47, and 16:1–8 writes an eyewitness signature to the whole narrative. Their presence as characters in the literary narrative testifies to the truth of these events in history.

The first written Gospel stands at a greater distance from the events of Jesus' life than the oral preacher and storytellers who handed on Jesus' good news orally for the forty years previous.[11] Their speaking could create the illusion of Jesus still speaking. Listeners could question them face to face about the message. In a written genre, the oral storyteller or preacher becomes an author who is concealed and anonymous in the text, implied by how the story is told but unavailable for questioning. Only the written story is available for communicating the message.

Speaking is an event in which experience comes to language, becomes something said—a repeatable, reidentifiable meaning. Even though the event of speaking slips past and falls silent, the words said can be remembered, distanced, and detached from the act of speaking. In face-to-face dialogue, the speaker remains immediately available to clarify what his or her words refer to—"No, it's not the road; it's the bridge that's out." Speakers can use their bodies, voices, faces, and objects to make their discourse clear to hearers. Speakers can refer back to what they said; hearers can refer the meaning they heard back to the speaker. Both can refer to objects in the situation. Face-to-face dialogue connects speaking and hearing and grounds reference in the situation.[12] The moment face-to-face dialogue ceases, interpretation becomes necessary. The hearer and reader must dialogue with the written story.

Writing distances something said from the speaker or author, from the situation, and from the original audience. Once written, however, something said can outlive and out-travel a speaker or author. Writing frees discourse from its reference to an immediate situation and projects its way-of-being-in-the-world toward an indeterminate audience. Distanced from the sources of its origin, the text becomes autonomous and available to all who can read. The written story offers its readers a description of a possible way-of-being-in-their-world that can enlarge their horizons of existence.[13]

Encoding in a genre further distances writing from face-to-face speaking. A written literary work encodes meaning in a genre, a publicly available system of processes and rules in the language, which an author with competence can produce and a reader with competence can interpret. Christians today inherit in the canon four works in the Gospel genre. The interpreter of Mark's Gospel, which is narrative in form, must be a reader or community of readers who can decode Mark's composition and rhetoric and respond to literary conventions such as plot, character, balance, symmetry, repetition, climax, contrast, ironic arrangement of events and characters, emphases at beginning and end, motifs, point of view, and tone. Children begin developing this competence at the age of reason.

As a written genre, the Markan narrative redescribes the events in history behind the text in order to create a narrative world that can communicate to an audience in front of the text the good news of Jesus Christ, the Son of God (1:1). Mark's Gospel does not record all that happened in Jesus' life or the disciples' experience but selects the disciples' fear, secrecy, and misunderstanding as controlling themes to communicate in its story world. "Narrative is the remaking of reality . . . through characterization, plot, and other narrative devices."[14] As a written work, the Gospel becomes a narrative world in itself, which addresses its christological truth claims to audiences in front of the text.

When Mary Magdalene, Mary the mother of James and Joses, and Salome enter Jesus' finished story to witness his death, burial, and resurrection, they inhabit the boundary of the narrative, where the text breaks into dialogue with the reader or hearer. After Jesus' death, the omniscient narrator pans back like a modern movie camera (15:39) to include eyewitnesses in the scene. The narrator identifies three women by name, who have followed and served Jesus in Galilee and come up with him to Jerusalem (15:41). Two of the women, Mary Magdalene and Mary the mother of Joses, see where Joseph of Arimathea buries Jesus' body (15:47). All three find Jesus' tomb empty three days later and hear a white-robed young man proclaim that Jesus is risen (16:1–8).

In their role as eyewitnesses the women disciples parallel the eyewitness function of the beloved disciple in John's Gospel. The beloved disciple is the intimate Jesus lets in on who will betray him. The beloved disciple stands with Jesus' mother, his mother's sister Mary the wife of Clopas, and Mary Magdalene at the cross. From the cross Jesus asks the beloved disciple to become Mary's child and to take Mary as a parent (19:25–27). The beloved disciple testifies that blood and water come from Jesus' side (John 19:34). The beloved disciple accompanies Peter and Mary Magdalene to the tomb that Mary has found empty (John 20:1–10); the beloved disciple enters the tomb, sees, and believes (20:8).

Like the three women witnesses in Mark's Gospel, the beloved disciple in John's Gospel witnesses Jesus' death and resurrection.

In John 19:35 and 21:20, 24, the omniscient narrator of the Fourth Gospel decloaks, acknowledging that the beloved disciple is not only a witness as a literary character but also the one who has written down this narrative and who puts an eyewitness signature on it to testify that the things written down in the Gospel are historically true. These verses don't identify the beloved disciple as the John who is one of Jesus' twelve. The implied author prefers the anonymous designation "beloved disciple" for the role of the eyewitness of Jesus' death and resurrection and the identified writer of the text.[15]

In Mark's Gospel, after the women witness Jesus' death, burial, and empty tomb, the narrative breaks off without their explicitly communicating their witness to anyone within the story. The reader or hearer, of course, learns the good news of Jesus' resurrection from the young man in the tomb along with the three women. In witnessing Jesus' death, burial, and empty tomb, the women write an implicit signature of eyewitness testimony to the whole text, just as does the eyewitness of the beloved disciple in John's Gospel. However, the women remain characters in the story. The text does not move them out of the narrative world to identify them with the implied author as the Fourth Gospel does the beloved disciple. Nonetheless, the fearful silence with which the text breaks off disengages the hearer or reader from the story world to assess the narrative and its claims as a whole, just as identifying the beloved disciple with the author in John 21:20, 24 disengages hearers and readers from the story and reminds them that the writing is a call to believe. The witness of the women signs the Gospel narrative; their silence allows the audience to hear the text and all it speaks as a call to faith and dialogue.

Within Mark's narrative, the women's silence echoes Jesus' provocative silence before the high priest and Pilate and his silent acceptance of the accusations passersby repeat as he hangs on the cross. When the women fall provocatively silent just when they should speak the news only they know, readers and hearers have the pieces to complete the puzzle. In this silence the truth claims of the narrative can echo in the hearer's mind and evoke a faith response.

The abrupt ending of the text creates a significant rhetorical and catechetical moment, a liminal space or threshold that hearers and readers must cross to faith in the risen Jesus. The women's silence draws the reader or hearer to ask, "But they must have told. If not, where did this story we just heard come from?" Indeed, although the women do not proclaim Jesus' resurrection to anyone in the narrative, the narrative itself proclaims the good news to hearers and readers. They hear the young man tell the women that Jesus is not in the tomb but risen and gone ahead of them to Galilee. As a written work that scholars date about 70 C.E., nearly two generations after Jesus' death and resurrection and just after the Roman destruction of the Second Temple in Jerusalem, the written Gospel itself provides the answer to the question its ending raises. The text in its entirety—its voice and concluding silence—calls a new generation of hearers to faith in its truth claims about Jesus. The suspended ending draws the reader or hearer back into the story. The story of Mark's Gospel drives forward from beginning to end; the discourse of Mark 16:1-8 drives backward from end to beginning.

Unlike the disciples in the story world, the hearers and readers of the Gospel don't need another verse to learn of Jesus' resurrection. The narrative is anything but silent about Jesus' resurrection. Three times Jesus prophesies his passion, death, and resurrection (8:31; 9:31; 10:33–34). These predictions vary but each ends identically, "and after three days he will rise again."[16] Jesus doesn't need to speak during his passion because he has prophesied all that happens. As he undergoes great suffering, is rejected by the elders, chief priest, and scribes (8:31), as he is betrayed into human hands (9:31), as he is handed over to the chief priest, condemned to death, handed over to the Gentiles, mocked, spat upon, flogged, and killed (10:33–34), Jesus' silence allows his predictions to re-echo as each plays out in the narrative. The women's silence at the end of the text functions the same way. It allows the good news the young man has just announced in the empty tomb to re-echo with Jesus' spoken prediction in 14:28, "After I am raised up, I will go ahead of you into Galilee," and with all three passion/resurrection predictions. The careful plotting of prophecy and silence sets the reader up to hear the echo of Jesus' words as his or her own response. The narrative drives forward beyond the text to the readers' faith and backward in the text to Jesus' words. The literary text carries out the commission the women do not fulfill.

The first Gospel doesn't narrate either Jesus' resurrection itself or an appearance of the risen Jesus. What fills the empty tomb is the young man's proclamation: "Jesus of Nazareth, the one who was crucified, is not here. He has been raised up." The written Gospel, a story written in language and inked on parchment, is one physical replacement of Jesus' absent body. As a written work, the Gospel from its beginning stands at a distance from Jesus' death and resurrection, not only in history but in reference. The Gospel is a source secondary to the events it recounts and to the testimony it hands on. However, this written work constructs a story that can migrate from its origins in Palestine, travel through time, and extend the promises of God to new generations all over the world. It constructs a movable literary world people can enter and share. As story and literary world, the Gospel refers forward to hearers and readers with whom it can communicate, and secondarily backward to events in Jesus' life. Certainly Mark anchors his Gospel in the life of the historical Jesus, and the other three Gospels replicate the essentials of his plot; but having become story, the Gospel has as its primary purpose communication, not documentation. The Gospel is rhetorical discourse whose primary purpose is to persuade its hearers to believe. Readers have direct, literary access to Mark's message in decoding the narrative's plot, characters, settings, rhetoric, and coherence but only secondary access to the historical Jesus and his first followers. Mark's text permanently scripts the empty tomb as liminal space and the women witnesses' silence as a threshold of dialogue between Jesus become story and all who hear this word.

In accepting Mark 16:8, as an artfully constructed turn to the audience, this literary-critical approach to reading Mark's Gospel heightens the role of the receivers of the Gospel. The real ending of Mark's Gospel is in the responses of its hearers. However, this literary-critical reading of the role of Markan women witnesses cannot stand without an accompanying feminist interpretation, for the three women who stand in silent awe at the empty tomb for a rhetorical reason are silenced in the tradition for patriarchal reasons. To construct a composite picture of what really happened in history, contemporary historical-critical inquiry tends to read Mark 16:8 in the light of the alternative ending of Mark and the Easter appearance narratives of Matthew, Luke, and John. At a very early stage these texts correct Mark's abrupt and dissatisfying ending and subordinate the witness of the women disciples to that of the male disciples, especially the eleven. In these other Gospels, the female proto-witnesses of Jesus' resurrection become messengers whose witness is important only in relationship to the male disciples, who become the credible witnesses of the resurrection and the proclaimers of the good news.

Scholarly interest in what really happened overlooks the most certain historical context in which people first heard Mark's Gospel—an intergenerational context. The fear and silence of the three faithful women witnesses is a rhetoric that addresses the next generation, the audience ahead of the text. It assumes that Mark's Gospel is a literary work, a world embodied within a written narrative, which readers can imagine and

interpret as their way of being-in-the-world. The Gospel text refers back-
wards to Jesus' life, as historical-critical research assumes. The Gospel
refers above all forward. Its small story units, its characters, its plot, its
setting, and its impact as a whole invite hearers and readers to respond to
its truth claims. With feminist interpretative principles that insist on keeping the three women witnesses at the center of interpretation, Mark 16:8
becomes a privileged site where silent foremothers call every next generation to speak their faith and join in the unfolding of Jesus' mission.

CHAPTER 3

Feminist Suspicion

When they heard that he was alive, and had been seen by her, they
would not believe it. (Mark 16:11)

THE WORD *FEMINIST* IDENTIFIES a method of biblical interpretation
that reads the silences and resists the biases that give Jesus' women
followers so little visibility in the traditions of Christian origins. The tools
for doing this feminist interpretative work are first critical, employing a
hermeneutic of suspicion; then, second, they are constructive, moving
women from the margins to the center in order to reclaim and make the
most of all that exists about women in the New Testament.[1] Feminist
interpreters of the New Testament want to recover women's place among
Jesus' disciples as a foundation for building communities of faith today
that welcome women's gifts as well as men's.

A feminist believes that women are full human persons, real people
who speak and act in history. A feminist is a man or woman who supports
and works for the full flourishing of women. The feminist practice in this
book joins the widening conversation with women of color and women
of the third world who struggle for just and equal systems and institutions
in our world and work to ensure that all can live.[2] In hearing silences and
bringing to light the barely visible, white feminist interpreters face their
own privilege and limitations and must welcome womanist, *mujerista*,
and third-world theologians who give voice to the injustices of their people and to their traditions of survival and sustenance. Jesus' women dis-

ciples in Mark's Gospel demonstrate some of the same energy to break
social boundaries and claim a fuller life that women seek in our time.

Hermeneutics is a word students always ask about in scripture classes.
What is it? How do you spell it? Why not use a word we all know?
Hermeneutics is the science and art of interpretation. The word comes
from the name Hermes, the Greek god with wings on his feet, who flew
back and forth among the other gods as their messenger. In the work of
interpretation, the mind must fly back and forth like Hermes between the
details of a work and its whole meaning, between the past of a work and
the present, between original meaning and contemporary readers.
Hermeneutics is the science and art of making conscious and explicit the
principles an interpreter uses to decode an ancient narrative such as
Mark's Gospel. What can this Gospel, written to proclaim the good news
of Jesus' resurrection to a first-century audience, say to us today? What
can women find in this first Gospel for their liberation today? Just as the
horizon changes as one drives across country, so the past as a horizon
changes from differing standpoints in the present.

> The historical movement of human life consists in the fact that it is never
> absolutely bound to any one standpoint, and hence can never have a truly
> closed horizon. The horizon is, rather, something into which we move and
> that moves with us. Horizons change for a person who is moving. Thus the
> horizon of the past, out of which all human life lives and which exists in the
> form of tradition, is always in motion. The surrounding horizon is not set
> in motion by historical consciousness. But in it this motion becomes aware
> of itself.[3]

Feminist biblical hermeneutics interprets scripture from new standpoints
and privileges voices that speak unheard differences.

The feminist hermeneutics with which this book examines Mark's
Gospel makes suspicion its first principle. A hermeneutic of suspicion is
an interpretative tool for recognizing and resisting androcentric and
patriarchal bias in the narrative. To put under suspicion is to put under
investigation, to question and reexamine, to dig deeper in hope of
unearthing new evidence and fuller truth. A hermeneutic of suspicion
questions the silences about women in the Gospel narratives. It suspects
that androcentric language and patriarchal social assumptions about what
and who are important obliterate women as agents in Christian tradition;
it suspects that the first Gospel minimizes women's participation in the
Jesus movement. Making a feminist critique of Mark's Gospel and its
interpreters is the work of this chapter.

HOW FEMINIST SUSPICION AROSE

Suspicion that God did not divinely sanction women's subordination arose in the United States as women joined in the struggle against slavery. They began to resist and prevail against the false assertion that God sanctions the system of slavery and intends the subordination of women.[4] In naming slavery an injustice and speaking their experience of this injustice, American abolitionist women such as Sarah Moore Grimké and Angelina Grimké came to recognize their own exclusion from suffrage, from church pulpits, and from the professions. The abolition movement began in New England in the 1820s and achieved its purpose in the United States with the Thirteenth Amendment to the Constitution on December 18, 1865. The Constitution enfranchised African-American men five years later with the Fifteenth Amendment. Women's suffrage did not follow until 1920 (the Twentieth Amendment).

Within the context of the continuing suffrage movement, Elizabeth Cady Stanton made a feminist critique of the Bible in 1895. Her *Woman's Bible* reinterprets the texts about women in the Old and New Testaments and establishes an agenda for feminist biblical hermeneutics.[5] She gathered and produced this "general and critical study of the Scriptures" because the opponents of women's emancipation repeatedly referred to the Bible as their authority. Cady Stanton insisted that women's subordinate place in society is not divinely ordained but wholly human in origin, inspired by the natural love of historians for domination.[6] Her work was controversial, even within the suffrage movement. In fact, so politically sensitive did her sister participants in the National American Suffrage Association find *The Woman's Bible* project that they voted to dissociate their organization from it despite Susan B. Anthony's stepping down from the chair and speaking for Cady Stanton. Cady Stanton acknowledged in her introduction to *The Woman's Bible* that women as well as men defend the authority of revelation and are the chief support of their subjugators.[7]

Other suspicions also originated in the nineteenth century with the rise of the individual, human rights, and democracy. Paul Ricoeur classifies the interpretative traditions of Marx, Nietzsche, and Freud as schools of suspicion.[8] These critical thinkers suspect that human consciousness distorts our individual and communal lives in systemic ways, privileging the elite classes and the conscious ego. In introducing the concept of illusion, Freud makes interpretation "no longer a matter of either error in the epistemological sense or lying in the moral sense, but illusion."[9] A hermeneutics of suspicion aims to demystify and reduce illusion, to dispossess people of naïve faith, heroic assumptions, and assumed values, but opens the way and even seeks a postcritical responsiveness to symbols and traditions.[10]

Simone de Beauvoir's analysis of woman as the *other* of man, who defines being human, is a classic concept that feminists use to identify the systemic distortion in male-constructed culture, thought, and language.[11] Women are objects; men, subjects. Women are passive; men, active agents. In all other relationships of domination, such as master/slave, employer/worker, rich/poor, majority/minority, imperial/colonial, or Christian/Jew, women are the other of the others.[12]

As the third millennium begins, women from around the globe continue the work of developing biblical hermeneutics that help liberate rather than subjugate women. Womanist, *mujerista*, Native American, and two-thirds-world theologians bring their own cultures and the needs of the people to Bible interpretation. As Chinese feminist theologian Kwok Pui-lan makes clear, "It is not enough to tell the history of how white women have developed a feminist critique of the Bible, without simultaneously telling the parallel of women of color. Our common heritage is our shared power."[13]

My own Scottish grandmother, Annie MacFarlane Mitchell, educated in the 1890s and active in rural Minnesota for women's suffrage, introduced me as a child to a hermeneutic of suspicion. Like all her grandchildren, I treasured the times she read from her soft-sueded leather book of Bobby Burns's poetry. My favorite was "To a Louse," in which a self-righteous woman in church can't see that a louse is crawling on the back of her hat and hair. "Ah, to see yourself as others see you," the poem ends. Put in the language of hermeneutics, every standpoint limits the possibility of vision.[14]

A feminist hermeneutic of suspicion schools Gospel readers to expect two systemic distortions in scriptural texts and in the history of their interpretation: first, the androcentric bias, which puts the male at the center of language and narrative; and second, the patriarchal bias, which puts the male at the top of the social order. Androcentric language renders women invisible and marginal as human subjects and agents in speech and written discourse by making the male the generic human and male experience the generic human experience.[15] Androcentric language uses the word *man* for *human*, *mankind* for *humankind*, and *he/his/him* as the third-person pronouns for men and for groups including men and women. The Greek and Hebrew languages have the same conventions in their usage. Writers in these languages use the male generic and male - pronouns for God, which means that not only our translations but also original texts have inscribed in them male-centered biases. Even though newswriters, educators, and publishers have embraced nonsexist, inclusive standards in their language usage, the language for naming and imaging God remains problematic for scholars who must deal with translations, for church officials who approve the texts for worship, and for individual Christians in their own imagining and reimagining of God. Probably few defenders of androcentric language for God actually think that God is literally male, but many men and women prefer to clothe God in male analogies and hold male imagery as foundational to personal faith or to church doctrine.

The Gospels are androcentric not only in their male-generic language conventions but also in their literary structure. Jesus, whom the Gospels proclaim is the Christ, is the male protagonist in each narrative. However, his character subverts his place at the center of the narrative. Jesus is not a world-conquering king but the crucified messiah with a message that he has come to serve rather than be served, to give his life rather than to take power, lord over others, and dominate. His message is not about his maleness but about God wanting our human wholeness; hence, he heals, forgives, and frees people, especially those regarded as outsiders in his society. Nonetheless, he all too easily becomes the heroicized focus of interpretation, commentary, and preaching. A feminist hermeneutic of suspicion resists privileging only Jesus in interpreting the narrative and examines as well the importance of the men and women disciples who follow Jesus, beginning in Mark 1:14–16 (Andrew, Peter, James, and John) and Mark 1:29–31 (Peter's mother-in-law), the roles of the women at the cross and empty tomb, and the roles of anonymous suppliants who will not keep Jesus' healing, freeing power secret.

To counter androcentric language we can use a conscious feminist interpretative principle that reads the Gospel narratives as inclusive of women until proven otherwise and that recognizes that generic male conventions of discourse do not mention women except when they become in some way problematic or exceptional.[16] The two verses about Jesus' women disciples (Mark 15:40–41) demonstrate the rightness of seeing women in the company of Jesus' disciples where language makes them invisible. These two verses not only place women who followed and served Jesus at his cross but retroject their presence throughout the preceding narrative. They had been with him in Galilee and had come up with him to Jerusalem. Chapter 5 explores the presence of the women of Galilee in the whole Gospel narrative.

A feminist hermeneutic of suspicion not only recognizes that androcentric language and discourse make women nearly invisible in gospel tradition but also expects to find in the scriptures patriarchal social assumptions that subordinate women to men. *Patriarchy,* which literally means "father rule," refers to any system of domination that constructs social pyramids on the basis of superiors and inferiors, definers and defined, male and female. Patriarchal oppression is

> a sociopolitical system and social structure of graded subjugations and oppressions. . . . Its classical expression is found in Aristotelian philosophy, which has decisively influenced not only Christian theology but also Western culture and political philosophy. Patriarchy defines not just women as the "other" but also subjugated peoples and races as the "other" to be dominated. It defines women, moreover, not just as the other of men but also as subordinated to men in power insofar as it conceives of society to be analogous to the patriarchal household, which was sustained by slave labor. Women of color and poor women are doubly and triply oppressed in such a patriarchal social system.[17]

Patriarchy names male-privileging social roles that many people unconsciously assume to be natural and God-given. Feminist hermeneutics insists that human beings construct male dominance through our social practices. In developing her feminist hermeneutics, Elisabeth Schüssler Fiorenza has elaborated the term *patriarchy* with its connotation of father rule over kin, by usefully inventing the term *kyriarchy,* the rule of lords and masters over ladies, minions, and slaves. In Greek *kyrios* means "lord," a title familiar from Christian liturgy. *Kyriarchy* names the systemic social practices of privileging men over women or any human over another for reasons of race, class, ethnic or cultural background, age, sexual preference, or religious affiliation. *Kyriarchy* is not a stable and static social pyramid but a dynamic practice of dominating that, when it interacts with gender, race, class, and culture, creates interlocking, multiple effects.[18]

> Simultaneous oppressions are not just multiple but multiplicative: racism is multiplied by sexism, multiplied by ageism, multiplied by classism, multiplied by colonial exploitation.[19]

We live in a dynamic social system, often complicit in lording or lady-

ing it over one another. In *kyriarchal* systems women get out of place easily, out of the established order. They were out of place publicly preaching against slavery and publicly seeking women's suffrage. The women's
movement continues to struggle with questions of place today. Is
women's place in the home, only in the home, or in whose home taking
care of whose kids? What place do women's gifts have in our communities of faith? Are women complementary to men or equal, or isn't there
a difference? The wedding vows most young couples exchange today do
not include, as they once did, a woman's promise to obey her husband.
Both men and women experience *kyriarchy* as dynamic, an ongoing system of some dominating others as they climb and construct social and
corporate pyramids.

Patterns of subordination exist in the Gospel narratives as they did in
the culture of Jesus' time and as they do today in ours. A feminist
hermeneutic of suspicion is a tool for the liberating democratic practice
of recognizing androcentric and patriarchal bias in sacred texts foundational to Christian communities today.

FEMINIST SUSPICIONS ABOUT THE FIRST GOSPEL

The women of Galilee who follow and serve Jesus in Mark 15:40–41
belong among the women whose presence the narrative minimizes and
the tradition, commentaries, lectionary, homilies, and catechetics usually
disregard. Only sixty of Mark's 660 verses feature women—10 percent.
The Markan narrative devotes only two verses to recognizing the presence of women among Jesus' disciples. In contrast, Jesus calls his first
men disciples—Peter, Andrew, James, and John—in 1:16–20, initiating
an overt presence of men disciples which extends through the narrative
until Judas exits with his betraying kiss in 14:45 and all but Peter flee at
Jesus' arrest (14:50). Peter extends the presence of men disciples in the
narrative as far as the high priest's courtyard, before the narrative suspends him in tearful regret as he realizes he has denied Jesus three times
as Jesus predicted (14:72). The women of Galilee, whom the omniscient
narrator/implied author keeps invisible in the story until 15:40 but who
15:41 tells us have followed and served Jesus from Galilee and come with
him to Jerusalem, are the most faithful disciples in the narrative, the story
characters who witness Jesus' death and burial, who find his tomb empty,
and who hear his resurrection proclaimed (15:40–41, 47; 16:1–8).

The Markan omniscient narrator, who can put words in Jesus' mouth and bring voices from heaven to speak in the text, selects the women disciples from Galilee to observe Jesus dead on the cross (15:40), to see where Joseph of Arimathea buries Jesus' body (15:47), and to find Jesus' tomb empty three days later (16:5–6). The three women disciples who enter Jesus' empty tomb (16:5) hear a young man proclaim that Jesus of Nazareth, who was crucified, has been raised and is no longer in the tomb. The women disciples are the omniscient narrator's eyewitnesses of Jesus' death, burial, and proclaimed resurrection. Through the voice of the young man, the omniscient narrator announces Jesus' resurrection and commissions the women (16:7) to tell Jesus' disciples and Peter that he has gone ahead of them to Galilee as he promised (14:28). Its rhetoric freezes the Markan narrative at the precise point where the women's next step requires active faith and willingness to proclaim the good news they have heard. At the conclusion of Mark's Gospel, only the omniscient narrator, the young man (the narrator's mouthpiece), and the women disciples know that Jesus is risen and goes ahead of his disciples to Galilee. However, ahead of the text are its hearers, who know what it proclaims and the resurrection faith it urges them to carry on. The women disciples open the door of the empty tomb for these hearers of the discourse. The women's silence in the story makes the final rhetorical move of the discourse, creating a silence that calls the reader to participate in interpreting the narrative and acting on its claims and call.

FEMINIST SUSPICIONS OF THE ALTERNATIVES
TO MARK'S ENDING

Mark 16:9–20

The rewritings of Mark's original ending subordinate the women disciples' testimony concerning Jesus' resurrection to the more credible and reliable witness of his male disciples. Although textual criticism can provide no evidence that Mark 16:9–20 was originally part of the Gospel, the modern translations of the Bible routinely continue to append Mark 16:9–20 as the or an ending of Mark. For example, one of the newest editions, the *New Oxford Annotated Bible*, New Revised Standard Version (1991) provides three endings of Mark's Gospel.

1. "THE SHORTER ENDING OF MARK," which begins "And all that had been commanded them they told briefly to those around Peter."

2. "THE LONGER ENDING OF MARK" (Mark 16:9–20).

3. A note after Mark 16:20 that provides in italics another ending, apocalyptic in tone, which other ancient authorities add in whole or in part following Mark 16:14.

Extended annotations beneath a fine line across the middle of the page discuss "The traditional close of the Gospel of Mark" with a presumption that the other appended endings indicate "that different attempts were made to provide a suitable ending for the Gospel." The notes grant that "it is possible that the compiler of the Gospel intended this abrupt ending" but "one can find hints that he intended to describe events after the resurrection: for example, Mark 14:28 looks forward to at least one experience of the disciples with Jesus in Galilee after the resurrection."[20]

Mark's Gospel acquires alternate endings early on, indicating that the ending is problematic; however, the visual placement of the endings on the page following Mark 16:8 and the notes show a bias toward the alternative ending as the more suitable one and suggest no reasons for the 16:8 ending. Both headings, however, presume that one or the other is the ending of Mark. *The Good News Bible, Today's English Version* labels these endings with less bias—"An Old Ending to the Gospel" and "Another Old Ending."[21] *The New American Bible* identifies the alternative endings as "The Longer Ending: 16,9–20," "The Shorter Ending," and "The Freer Logion." It notes concerning Mark 16:8, "Mark's composition of the gospel ends at 16,8 with the women silenced by the mystery."[22] The interpretation, even if one differs with its conclusions, at least suggests a positive value in the original ending. The other notes, especially those of the *New Oxford Annotated Bible,* reflect a historical-critical bias toward using subsequent Synoptic tradition to correct Mark's original ending. The alternative endings erase the women's significance in the original.

The alternative ending in Mark 16:9–20 begins with a clue that it was never part of the original. Mark 16:9 needlessly reestablishes the time, "Now after he rose on the first day of the week," a time already established in Mark 16:2. The ending appends three appearance stories to the apparently unsatisfactory empty tomb story of Mark 16:1–8, three accounts in carefully crafted interrelationship.[23] In the first account "those who had been with Jesus" refuse to believe the testimony of Mary Magdalene that Jesus lives. In the second appearance story they refuse to believe the witness of two disciples whose gender is not specified. These rejections set up the third appearance as significant and climactic. Those who experience the third appearance become the most credible witnesses of Jesus' risen presence. The third appearance is, of course, to Jesus' male disciples.

Although Mary Magdalene remains the first to see Jesus risen in the alternative ending in Mark 16:9–20, the other disciples' refusal to believe her undermines her witness as does the way this ending characterizes her.

> Now after he rose early on the first day of the week, he appeared first to Mary Magdalene, from whom he had cast out seven demons. She went out and told those who had been with him, while they were mourning and weeping. But when they heard that he was alive and had been seen by her, they would not believe it. (Mark 16:9–11)

These verses repeat a detail only Luke provides about Mary Magdalene—the seven demons (Luke 8:2). Being freed of seven demons ought to be a convincing Christian credential. Rita Nakashima Brock maintains "exorcism stories use demons to depict the loss of self-possession."[24] She brings this concept together with the insight from conscientization that the subordinated internalize the negative and destructive self-concepts of those who dominate them.[25] On these terms the character borrowed for Mary Magdalene suggests a woman in full possession of herself rather than the once-unstable and therefore less-than-trustworthy witness the other disciples disregard. The second story in the series of three (16:12) also borrows from Luke; it recounts that Jesus appeared to two disciples as they are walking into the country, a story similar to Luke's story of two disciples recognizing the risen Jesus when they eat with him on their way home to Emmaus. In Mark 16:13, no one believes them, "And they went back and told the rest, but they did not believe them" (16:13).

The *New American Bible* translates this verse, "but the others put no more faith in them than in Mary Magdalene," although the Greek text of v. 13 does not mention Mary Magdalene (*oude ekeinois episteusan*). The *New American Bible* makes Mary's testimony a standard of incredulity over against which the eleven have to see for themselves.

When in the third story Jesus appears to the eleven (16:14), he chides them for refusing to believe the earlier witnesses and substantiates the truth of these earlier testimonies. Nonetheless, only the eleven become believing and credible witnesses whom Jesus sends out to proclaim the good news to all creation (16:15–20). This alternative ending to Mark shows a bias against Mary Magdalene's witness and a bias toward the eleven's testimony.

Matthew and Luke

Robert M. Fowler terms Matthew and Luke early readers of Mark who respond to the Gospel's rich ambiguities and ironies by retelling the story with ambiguities clarified and ironies dissolved.[26] These earliest interpreters of Mark's Gospel both append appearances of the risen Jesus to Mark's empty tomb story and, in doing so, subordinate and discount the women's witness. Matthew and Luke's rewritings show an androcentric and patriarchal bias that prefers male disciples as reliable witnesses of the news that Jesus is risen and subordinates the women's testimony to the men's.

At the end of Matthew's Gospel Mary Magdalene and Mary the mother of James and Joseph find the tomb empty and hear the Easter kerygma from an angel. Matthew elaborates Mark's narrative, mitigating the women's fear and silence into a temporary state of half joy and half fear which they feel as they go to tell Jesus' disciples that he will see them in Galilee. In 28:9–10 Jesus himself appears to the women, who respond in worship and touch his feet. Jesus tells the women not to be afraid and repeats the angel's commission to tell his brothers. The Matthean discourse reinforces the women's importance by having Jesus appear to them before anyone else; however, Matthew at the same time subordinates their importance as preachers by having Jesus also commission them to tell his brothers. Matthew makes specific that the women tell Jesus' brother disciples; in Mark the young man commissions the women to tell "his disciples and Peter" (16:7). Readers know from Mark 15:41 and Matthew 27:55–56 that Jesus has many women disciples. Matthew's Gospel creates a climactic commissioning scene to end its narrative. In this scene Jesus appears specially to the eleven male disciples on the same mountain in Galilee where he called them and commissions them "to make disciples of all nations" (28:19). The women in Matthew become messengers to the male disciples rather than proclaimers to the world. Matthew regards both the Markan empty tomb and the women's concluding fear and silence as insufficient testimony to Jesus' risen presence. Matthew adds appearance narratives to assure Jesus' presence more explicitly and makes the eleven Jesus' only credible witnesses.

Luke retells Mark's empty tomb story with some elaboration (24:1–9) but does not name the women until v. 10 as the ones who hear the kerygma from two angels and then report their experience to the eleven and the others; then he names Mary Magdalene, Joanna, and Mary the mother of James and mentions that others with them told the story. No one believes the women (24:11), so Peter goes to the tomb, finds it empty, and returns amazed. The women's witness is disregarded until Peter substantiates it.

John

John's Gospel condenses into two verses (20:1–2) Mary Magdalene's finding the tomb open, running to get Peter and the beloved disciple, and suggesting that Jesus' body has been taken from the tomb. The empty tomb contains folded grave cloths but no young man or angels who proclaim the good news, which eliminates Mary Magdalene's role as the first to hear the good news of Jesus' resurrection. Peter and the beloved disciple are the only ones to enter the tomb; they find it empty, eclipsing Mary's role in the Synoptic Gospels as the one who enters the tomb. Rather, the beloved disciple, who is also the implied author of John, becomes the second to see the empty tomb and the first to believe. However, John's Gospel does feature Mary Magdalene in the second of the four appearance stories it recounts in John 20. The first appearance narrative focuses on the beloved disciple (vv. 1–10), the second on Mary Magdalene (vv. 11–18), the third on the fearful community (vv. 19–23), and the fourth on doubting Thomas (vv. 24–31). John's Gospel preserves a woman among its models of Easter faith.

Historical-Critical Interpreters

The way Matthew, Luke, and John retell and seemingly correct Mark colors the ways historical-critical commentators interpret the women's importance. For example, C. F. D. Moule, in a short study of Mark 16:8, proposes understanding the women's saying nothing to anyone (*oudeni ouden eipan*) as parenthetical. No one, he maintains, would puzzle over the women's fear and silence as a temporary state that they experienced as they ran straight back to the disciples refusing to greet anyone on the way. He reinterprets the puzzle of Mark 16:8 in the light of Matthew, presuming that the second Gospel provides additional information about what happened in history rather than considering Mark 16:8 as a purposeful ending.[27]

The longer alternative ending of Mark and the three retellings of Jesus' story in the gospel genre minimize, eclipse, or trivialize the significance

Mark's narrative gives to Mary Magdalene and the other women witnesses of the good news that Jesus is risen. Not only does the continuing
early gospel tradition erode the women disciples' reliability as witnesses
of Jesus' resurrection, but historical-critical perspectives today collude
with these texts to reconstruct what happened behind the text. Like
Moule and the notes in the *New Oxford Annotated Bible*, most historical-
critical study accepts the Markan narrative as but one source among the
other Gospels and other New Testament sources for constructing a composite picture of what really happened on Easter morning. This move
subordinates the three women witnesses of Jesus' good news to the male
disciples and makes Mary Magdalene's testimony a standard of
incredulity. It removes the role of women as exemplary first-generation
disciples whose rhetorical silence calls next-generation hearers to act. The
appearance narratives of the other three Gospels de-emphasize the empty
tomb story with its appeal to reader response and provide assurances of
Jesus' resurrection that finish the Gospel within the text rather than with
a deliberate uptake that calls for audience faith.

Gnostic Gospels

Gnostic literature of the first, second, and third centuries includes Mary
Magdalene among disciples who talk with Jesus and, in the case of the
Gospel of Mary, receive special knowledge from him after his resurrection.
Many of these writings are postresurrection dialogues with the risen
Jesus. Few samples of ancient Gnostic writing were available to scholars
until the discovery of about fifty tractates near Nag Hammadi in Egypt in
1945 and their publication more than thirty years later.[28] Among these
writings, the *Gospel of Thomas* and the *Gospel of Mary* suggest conflict
between Mary Magdalene and Peter.

The *Gospel of Thomas* is a sayings collection, probably begun in the first
century and concluded before the middle of the second.[29] Both Mary
Magdalene and Salome are among the disciples in the *Gospel of Thomas*
who ask Jesus questions, Mary Magdalene in logia 21 and 114, Salome
in logion 61. Both women are ordinary disciples in this Gospel; Thomas,
the one spiritually advanced. Although the *Gospel of Thomas* keeps Mary
Magdalene and Salome among Jesus' inner circle as peers, it reveals controversy about women's leadership in Peter's concluding request, "Let
Mary leave us, for women are not worthy of Life."[30] Jesus himself counters Peter's request and takes personal responsibility for making Mary
male.

I myself shall lead her in order to make her male, so that she too may
become a living spirit resembling you males. For every woman who will
make herself male will enter the Kingdom of Heaven. (*Gospel of Thomas*
114)

"Making oneself male" has three lines of interpretation.[31] First, it may
mean cutting one's hair short and accepting male dress, signifying a radical ascetic choice that excludes one from marriage, childbearing, and
hence sexual life. Thecla, in the *Acts of Paul and Thecla,* offers one spir-
ited example of this choice. When Paul will not baptize her so she can
preach, she baptizes herself in a pool of seals and later helps found a community of women.[32] Schüssler Fiorenza refers to such choices as Thecla's
as "role revolt."[33] Second, making oneself male may refer to the Platonic
myth of the androgyne or to the pristine, pre-fall state of humankind.
Third, the transformation from female to male suggests moving from all
that is earthly, sensual, imperfect, and passive to all that is transcendent,
chaste, perfect, and active.[34] Although Gnostics see both men and women
having to make this transformation from female to male, the terminology
uses the patriarchal assumption of female inferiority. Both Jesus and Peter
use this patriarchal language.[35] Unlike New Testament traditions, the
Gospel of Thomas maintains Mary Magdalene's place in the community.[36]

The *Gospel of Mary*, like the *Gospel of Thomas*, a postresurrection dialogue between Jesus and his disciples, also describes a conflict between
Mary Magdalene and Peter. The beginning and end of this Gospel are
missing. Shortly after the extant manuscript begins, the risen Jesus leaves
the disciples, who despair.

> How shall we go to the gentiles and preach the gospel of the kingdom of
> the true human being? If they did not spare him [Jesus], how will they
> spare us? (9.7–12)

Mary Magdalene, who is the beloved and spiritually advanced disciple[37] in this Gospel, comforts her despondent male colleagues and turns
their minds to the good (9.14–22), to the root in them of their spiritual
origins. Then Peter addresses Mary as an equal with the term "sister" and
acknowledges her special relationship to Jesus, "Sister, we know that the
Savior loved you more than the rest of women" (10.1–2). Peter asks
Mary to tell the group other words she has heard from the Savior that
they have not heard. Mary speaks of continuing visions of Jesus, hidden
from the others but from which she does not waver (10.5–10). After
Mary speaks, Andrew and Peter question whether the Savior "really
spoke privately to a woman and not openly to us?" "Did he prefer her to

us?" they ask (17.15–20). "Do you think that I thought this up myself in my heart, or that I am lying about the Savior?" (18.1–5), she replies. These Gnostic Gospels amplify the tension in the canonical Gospels about the credibility of Mary Magdalene. Elaine Pagels sees political implications in these tensions that suggest "whoever 'sees the Lord' through inner vision can claim that his or her own authority equals, or surpasses, that of the twelve—and of their successors."[38] Pagels argues that the controversy concerning the experience of the risen Jesus in these Gnostic Gospels and the orthodox teaching on resurrection "legitimized a hierarchy of persons through whose authority all others must approach God."[39] Karen King also hears a crisis of authority behind the conflict in the *Gospel of Mary* between Peter and Mary. She notes that all legitimate authority in early Christianity appeals to Jesus' words and deeds.[40] In having Jesus affirm Mary's teaching and leadership role against Peter's charge that the Savior would not tell her things he did not tell the men disciples, the *Gospel of Mary* affirms the legitimacy of women's apostolic leadership.

> Mary, along with Levi, represents those Christians who question the validity of any apostolic authority that challenges the truth of their own experience of the living Lord; for them, apostolic authority is not based on being one of the Twelve or one gender but on spiritual qualifications. Women who have those qualifications may exercise legitimate authority.[41]

All four Gospels and this Gnostic literature include the women as the first witnesses of the empty tomb and the good news of Jesus' resurrection. This consistency argues that their presence at the tomb is a non-negotiable part of tradition and therefore makes probable that women were part of what happened. Their subordination in the tradition, then, provides evidence of patriarchal discourse in the handing on of tradition. In the canonical tradition, the good news of Jesus' resurrection has to be more than a woman's tale to be believed and only male disciples receive explicit commissions to preach to the nations. The *Gospel of Mary* affirms women's spiritual leadership in the second century but shows it to be controversial. Always in Gnostic tradition Mary Magdalene is a disciple and spiritual leader, not the prostitute of later Gospel interpretation.[42]

The Lectionary: The Gospel We Proclaim Today

This marginalizing of women in the Gospel traditions continues in contemporary proclamation, as organized in the current Roman Catholic

Sunday lectionary, *Book of Gospels*,[43] which for the most part follows the common lectionary that Episcopalians, Lutherans, Methodists, and Presbyterians use. For Easter Sunday in each of three lectionary cycles, the church reads John's story of Mary Magdalene running to get Peter and the other disciple when she finds the tomb empty (John 20:1–9). For the Second Sunday of Easter in each cycle, the church reads the story of Jesus appearing to the whole community and then to Thomas (John 20:19–31). Although the Second Vatican Council mandated expanding the lectionary from one to three cycles of readings in order to set the table of the Word with richer scriptural fare,[44] the Gospels for Easter and the Second Sunday of Easter each year read John 20:1–9 and John 20:19–31, respectively, excluding John 20:10–18, the story of Mary Magdalene meeting Jesus in the garden near the empty tomb.[45] The lectionary does allow reading the Gospel for the Easter Vigil as an alternative to John on Easter Sunday. In cycle B, this reading is Mark 16:1–7, a shortening of the final pericope of Mark's Gospel that creates yet another alternative ending of Mark's Gospel. Ending the Easter Gospel at Mark 16:7 eliminates the troublesome fear and silence of the women disciples and orients the narrative to Jesus and his promise that his disciples will see him in Galilee (16:7).

The lectionary reads the verses about the women of Galilee at the cross and tomb on Passion Sunday from Matthew 27:55–56, 61 in cycle A; from Mark 15:40–42, 47 in cycle B; from Luke 23:49 in cycle C. The short forms of these Gospels end before the women enter the narrative in cycles A and B; the cycle-C short form makes the women and other observers the concluding verse of the story. The two verses about Jesus' women disciples in Mark and Matthew and the one verse in Luke compete with Jesus' whole passion for public hearing in contemporary church worship. The case is the same for another woman's story, that of an unnamed woman's anointing of Jesus' head, which begins the passion story in Mark (Mark 14:3–9). This story comes in the early verses of the cycle-B Gospel for Passion Sunday. Schüssler Fiorenza points out in the introduction to *In Memory of Her* that tradition remembers the name of the disciple who betrayed Jesus, the name of the disciple who denied him, and the names of those who fled his arrest, but not the name of the woman who prophetically recognized and anointed Jesus for burial at the second to the last supper before he was arrested, suffered, and died. Schüssler Fiorenza names her work on the feminist theological reconstruction of Christian origins for this woman, whose story Jesus directs should be told in her memory wherever the good news is proclaimed.

Schüssler Fiorenza notes that the Markan text intercuts this woman's prophetic anointing between 14:1–2, in which the chief priests and scribes look for a way to arrest and kill Jesus, and 14:10–11, in which Judas, one of Jesus' own disciples, goes to the leaders to betray Jesus. This intercut makes the women's example stand out, as does Jesus' affirmation of her act (14:8). Yet Christians who regularly obey Jesus' command to break bread and pour out wine in his memory, rarely obey his command to tell this woman's story wherever the good news is told.[46]

Mark 16:9–20, Matthew 28, Luke 24, and John 20 silence the purposeful rhetoric that ends the first Gospel with the narrative's most faithful disciples fixed in fear and silence. Tradition marginalizes these sentinels, whose silence once pressed hearers to speak their own faith.

CHAPTER 4

Liberating Reading

ॐ

FOLLOWING A SUSPICIOUS READING of the Gospel (a critical phase of interpretation), feminist hermeneutics moves women in the narrative from the margin to the center, a constructive phase of interpretation. Like a musical score, the Gospel must be interpreted and performed. To perform the Gospel as liberating proclamation for people in our world today is the aim of feminist biblical interpretation. This includes reconstructing women's place in Christian origins, rereading and decoding the truth claims of the literary narrative, and welcoming readers from new social locations to dialogue with the story and generate new speech about its meaning.

The study in this book combines feminist, literary, and liberation hermeneutics to do the constructive work of rereading Mark's Gospel as a liberating narrative for today. First, a feminist hermeneutic shifts the women in Mark 16:1–8 from the margin of the text and interpretation to the center.

Second, a literary-critical approach views the first Gospel as a literary rather than a historical work, as a mirror in which an audience might find reflected its way to be in the world rather than as a window on the past. Historical-critical study regards Mark's Gospel as one primary source among others to use in constructing a composite picture of what really happened in Jesus' life and ministry in history. For the past two hundred years this approach has employed its tools to clean away the accumulated smudge of centuries of interpretation and reclaim the original genius of Jesus. The dialogue that historical-critical study seeks is with Jesus in history. The dialogue the first Gospel narrative seeks as a literary work is not with the past but with an audience ahead of the text in the future. In composing a narrative, an author structures the plot, characters, setting, and themes to engage and have an effect on an audience. Authors plot mysteries to keep readers in suspense. Homer begins the *Odyssey* with scenes that show Odysseus's wife, Penelope, holding off suitors and his son setting off to find his father before the poet washes the hero himself ashore on a nearby island and lets him tell his whole story. In its use of narrative form, the Gospel does not aim to entertain and delight like an epic or a mystery but to proclaim who Jesus is and persuade readers of its claims.

Third, a liberation hermeneutic shifts who makes meaning from the author interpreting history to the reader's generative role in interpreting text. Historical criticism seeks to document what in the Gospel narratives can be verified as historically true or at least probable. It seeks what the text meant originally. Literary criticism explores the world of the text itself. It bases interpretation on what characters say and do in the story, on how the author arranges them, on how repeated images and themes interpret the narrative from within itself, prestructuring meaning for readers. A liberation hermeneutic privileges the social location of people on the margins as sites from which to interpret the Gospel for today. It values what readers in every age, from every culture and race, of both genders bring to reading. These are the readers who read from their own experience in our world and for the life and liberation of its people. The reader affects the read. This makes who decides what the Gospel means an issue.

With these three shifts in focus, the first Gospel is no longer only about Jesus back then and the men he trained to take his place. It is about all the women and men disciples and suppliants in the narrative and about all of us who receive and read this narrative today.

What we see depends on where we stand.[1] No one can interpret without becoming part of the interpretation. Our questions and experience shape the interpretation we construct. My own social location shows in my interpretation of Mark 16:8. As a feminist, I see this verse as a site of resistance to silencing and trivializing the three women disciples. As a practicing writer highly trained in literature and literary criticism, I see in this final verse of the first Gospel a literary prism for interpreting the whole narrative and a rhetorical strategy for turning to a new generation. As a member of the Roman Catholic Church, a Sister of St. Joseph, and a lifelong minister of the word in the catechetical field, I see in Mark 16:8 three women whose witness models faith and leadership for Christian

women today. I see the empty tomb and the women's fear and silence as
a liminal threshold where proclamation invites new hearers to faith.
Lastly, as a white woman committed to just and inclusive community on
this planet, I see in Mark 16:8 the generative boundary of the narrative
that invites readers and hearers to dialogue with the story from their
social locations and perform the Gospel for the liberation and life of us
all.

FEMINIST HERMENEUTIC OF HISTORICAL RECONSTRUCTION

My rereading of the first Gospel in the light of Mark 16:8 builds on the
work of Elisabeth Schüssler Fiorenza but adapts her historical-critical
principles of interpretation to a literary-critical approach. In her 1985
book *In Memory of Her*, Schüssler Fiorenza set out to restore women to
the history of Christian origins and the history of Christian beginnings to
women.[2] She combines feminist and historical-critical tools to create feminist hermeneutics of historical reconstruction for breaking the silence of
texts about women and recovering clues about their participation as subjects in the Jesus movement. Her methodology includes such working
principles as the following:

1. Shift women from margin to center of interpretation in order to
   reverse the marginalizing perspective of patriarchal tradition and
   interpretation.[3]

2. Assume that patriarchal history is women's history too. Reclaim
   Christian history as women's own past and preserve the memory of
   suffering, defeat, and struggle as well as power.[4]

3. Assume that any textual mention of women represents a more
   extensive presence in history.[5]

4. Use women's social history research to counter and reimagine the
   objectification of women in roles or types (the sinner or prostitute)
   or assumptions that women are dependent or derivative of men.
   Challenge passages that trivialize or ridicule women.[6]

5. Read rules that seek to silence or control women as evidence that
   women are speaking and acting as subjects and not necessarily com-
   plying with rules.[7]

6. Uncover and reject in the scriptures "all that perpetuates in the name of God, violence, alienation, and patriarchal subordination of women."[8]

7. Use egalitarian-inclusive passages within the canonical texts to critique passages that place women in secondary status.[9]

When Schüssler Fiorenza uses her hermeneutics of historical reconstruction to examine Mark 16:8, she refuses to recognize the women disciples' fear and silence as a permanent state in the historical world behind the text. She wants to reclaim the women as faithful rather than failed witnesses. With German feminist Luise Schottroff she suggests that the women's fear reflects the fears of the community for whom Mark writes.[10] Schottroff observes that the women's heightened fear and awe-filled silence are unique to Mark's telling of the Gospel story and infers that Mark must have written for a community experiencing fear. These interpretations put positive value on the women witnesses' role in the Gospel, but neither looks at this verse that originally ended the first Gospel as a generative literary site from which to reread the whole narrative.

FEMINIST LITERARY HERMENEUTICS

The Gospels have reference not only to the real historical events behind the text; they also have inner systems of reference. Each of the four Gospels is a literary whole, an artfully coherent composition in which plot, character, motif, setting, and patterns of arrangement work together toward an intended response from hearers and readers. This means that the characters, their feelings, and the setting in Mark 16:8 have reference to other parts of the narrative whole. In addition to its reference to events in history behind the text and to the self-contained narrative world of the text, each Gospel also addresses an audience ahead of the text.[11] Each claims that Jesus is the messiah and functions rhetorically to persuade hearers and readers to believe in Jesus, whom God raised from the dead.

This study combines feminist-critical principles of interpretation with literary-critical and rhetorical analysis to explore what the first Gospel communicates when we look at it through the prism of the women disciples' fear and silence in its final verse. Besides moving some of Schüssler Fiorenza's hermeneutics of historical reconstruction into a literary context, the feminist literary interpretive practices in this study draw on

Rebecca Chopp's insistence on privileging otherness and difference in feminist discourse[12] and on Mieke Bal's analysis of male ideology embedded in narrators' points of view.[13] These feminist literary hermeneutics include the following principles:

1. Move women to the center of interpretation. Privilege women characters—their voices, actions, and significance in story and discourse.

2. Privilege details that characterize women as subjects. Question and counter the objectifying, trivializing, or ridiculing of women characters.

3. Challenge the inferior status of women characters or other "others" defined in categories such as possessed, sinful, nameless, poor, suppliant.

4. Privilege narrative evidence that expresses the experience of women and counters the subordination of women characters and their dependence on or derivation from men characters.

5. Challenge the use of Jesus' voice to give authority to teachings that lack congruence with his whole message.

6. Analyze the omniscient narrator's viewpoint for its relationship to women. Analyze who speaks in the narrator's voice and tone.

As I used literary analysis to examine the motifs of fear and silence throughout the first Gospel, I noticed in doing this work that Mary Magdalene, Mary the mother of James and Joses, and Salome form a character group of three parallel to the male trio Peter, James, and John. I further discovered that the three men disciples are as silent about who Jesus is as the women. Neither trio of well-known, named characters ever tells in the Gospel the secret that Jesus is the messiah. Mark has constructed the first Gospel so that all the disciples who knew Jesus face to face, who accompanied him in his ministry, and then went with him to Jerusalem and his death are silent, both the women and the men.

THE ORIGINAL RHETORICAL CONTEXT

Why characterize the men and women eyewitnesses in fear and silence? Why such a negative tone in the attitude of the author toward these characters? These questions led me to think rhetorically about the audience for whom the author of the first Gospel wrote. Jesus' death and resurrection are forty years in the past. His disciples have spread the gospel throughout the Mediterranean world during the intervening decades; in fact, Jesus' disciples would be between sixty and eighty years old at the time Mark wrote.

At this point I began to draw a time line with 30 C.E., the approximate year of Jesus' death and resurrection, at the left and the date of the writing of the Gospel, 70 C.E., at the right end of the line. I added a line to create an angle, a vector extending in time from the redeeming event of Jesus' death and resurrection outward, indicating the spread of the gospel. I drew a dashed line vertically through the angle at 70 C.E. I saw two generations of Christians between the dates—an eyewitness generation of disciples who knew Jesus and continued his mission and a second generation who knew the eyewitnesses and came to faith on their word. I realized that by 70 C.E. the community needed the written Gospel to stabilize and continue the eyewitnesses' testimony.

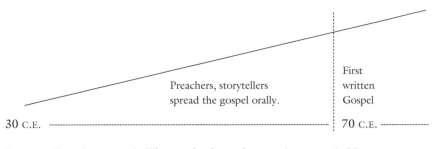

Preachers, storytellers
spread the gospel orally.

First
written
Gospel

30 C.E. -- 70 C.E. ----------------

Jesus * Eyewitnesses * Those who hear the eyewitnesses * New era

Figure 1

To establish a feel for this intergenerational time frame, return with me to the twentieth century. At the time I was doing this research and interpretation, our next-door neighbors, LaRue and Newman, began attending fifty-year reunions of their World War II army units. The year 1995 marked the fiftieth anniversary of the end of World War II. Newman and LaRue seldom come over for dinner without sharing with us stories of their participating in this war. Newman fought with General Patton up from Italy into France and through the freezing cold of the Battle of the Bulge. "We was dug into the snow and trying to keep warm. A week it went on. They had us pinned down pretty good, too." A private like Newman tells a different view of war than most history books. He admired Patton for never putting his men in unnecessary danger. He got a fresh uniform after months in the same one when he was selected to appear with Patton in a review. I can tell these oral traditions because I've heard them often, each time from the engaging eyewitness next door.

LaRue, an army nurse, took part in the liberation of Paris. A hospital across the city from where she was stationed notified her that her brother had been brought in wounded, but she couldn't get to him because she was working around the clock with the number of wounded coming to her hospital. Someone delivered her brother to her hospital in an ambulance that night. She often recounts this and other profound experiences of shared purpose in this war.

Once when Newman and LaRue joined us for Thanksgiving, we also entertained a young couple from Belgium. As Newman and LaRue told their stories, these young people felt oddly at home. "Our grandparents tell these same stories," they said.

Fifty years after World War II people still have access to firsthand personal accounts of their parents' or grandparents' participation in the war. If these memories are to be preserved, however, they have to be written down soon because our neighbors are in their eighties.

To return from this contemporary example back to the first century, the year 70 C.E. is especially pivotal in Christian history because it marks a decade when most eyewitnesses of Jesus' ministry, death, and resurrection have already died or have grown vulnerably old and because the Romans destroy Israel's temple that year. After this, neither Jews who follow Jesus nor other Jews have any way to return to the temple-centered religion of the past with its pilgrimages for feasts, prayer, incense, and sacrifices.

Concurrently with the four-year Jewish rebellion that ended in the Romans' destruction of the temple, Nero persecuted Christians in Rome, putting to death in the late 60s C.E. Peter and Paul, two of the Christian community's strong leaders. Rhetorically, the first written Gospel addresses an audience of people who never knew Jesus face to face, who did know that his eyewitness disciples had given their lives to spreading the gospel, and who have good reason to fear making a similar commitment.

What if, I theorized, the woman disciples of Mark 16:8 were as well known in the early Christian communities as Peter, James, and John? What if people in 70 C.E. knew that the women, like the men disciples, had given their lives to spreading the gospel and sustaining the new community? The author of Mark could then presume that the audience knew the women weren't silent in history and could recognize their literary silence as contrary to fact and a call to take their places. Several non-canonical Gnostic sources give Mary Magdalene and other women leadership roles among Jesus' disciples.[14] The canonical Gospels, however, provide readers with no additional information about Mary Magdalene's missionary activity as they do for Peter. A contemporary audience in 2000 C.E. knows no reason not to accept their silence as factual. The canon puts us contemporary readers in a different relation to Peter. When Mark's Gospel suspends Peter in tears at the high priest's courtyard, realizing and regretting that he has just denied Jesus, we readers today don't hear his silence. We know from other New Testament sources that Peter becomes a preacher of Jesus' message. He is not silent in history, but Mark deliberately has him fall silent in the first Gospel. Perhaps the author of Mark deliberately has the best-known men and women disciples fall silent as characters in the Gospel because they are dead or aging, no longer able to proclaim to another generation in history who Jesus is. In order to call a new generation to discipleship, the first Gospel characterizes Jesus' eyewitness disciples not as the heroic missionaries they became as they gave their lives to preaching the good news, but as they were at the beginning of their discipleship, afraid and amazed, like the women at the empty tomb.

In fact, in the final chapter of Mark's Gospel, Jesus is absent, risen, and gone ahead to Galilee as he promised. This scene, written for an audience forty years after Jesus' death and resurrection, puts at center stage three women who followed Jesus during his ministry and in all likelihood continued to follow and serve the Christian community during the forty years between Jesus' resurrection and the writing of the first Gospel. The growing body of research interpreting the first-, second-, and third-century Gnostic writings unearthed at Nag Hammadi in Egypt in 1945 shows Mary Magdalene as an active disciple and enlightened teacher, controversial because of her gender and gifts for leadership.[15] Although the *Gospel of Thomas* and the *Gospel of Mary*, both of which suggest conflict, may be dated as early as the first half of the second century (100–150 C.E.), scholars can only wonder if the controversy over women's leadership in the Gnostic communities echoes earlier conflict in Christian communities between 70 and 100 C.E. If such proof existed, it might argue that the suspended ending of Mark's Gospel represents a historical silencing rather than a rhetorical strategy. On the other hand, the aging of the eyewitness generation is as certain as actuarial tables. In 30 C.E., the approximate time in history when the events in the Gospel take place,

Mary the mother of James and Joses has grown sons, so she must be thirty-five years old. This makes her seventy-five at the time of the writing of the first Gospel forty years later. Mary Magdalene and Salome may have been younger in 30 C.E., but if they were twenty years old then, they are sixty at the time the author of Mark writes. In 70 C.E., a written Gospel begins to do the work that eyewitnesses who remain alive are growing too old to do—calling others to voice as believers.

HERMENEUTICS FOR LIBERATING DIALOGUE
WITH THE NARRATIVE

Jesus' words and actions become story in the first Gospel. An author gives them a literary form that allows them to travel through time and space to deliver Jesus' message and the witness of his first followers. Toward that purpose, the Gospel addresses hearers and readers ahead of it in time. It addresses us today among those hearers and readers.

When we receive the Gospel narrative, we are no longer in the same place as the original audience for whom Mark wrote. Our lives are not at risk in believing, although in some cases they may be. We live in a world that is celebrating two millennia of successive generations following Jesus' way and having effect in our world. Slavery appalls us, but women's equality with men remains a brutal tension among us. Feminists as a community of readers today use principles of interpreting that facilitate liberating dialogue with the ancient story, freeing its truth for our lives by speaking the truth of our lives to it. As Elaine Wainwright observes, "The interpretive process is not one way; it takes place in the interstices between questions brought to the text and those the text asks of the reader."[16]

A feminist hermeneutic of liberation "listens" the religious experience of women today into words that can dialogue with the Gospel narrative, claim its emancipatory truth, and transform its bias. In this approach, social location becomes more than a standpoint to acknowledge in scholarly work and more than a site of resistance to all discourse that does not speak women's truth; it becomes generative space from which new voices and new speech can transform and liberate the Gospel's meaning. Social location connotes more than this analytical term defines. It is the very ground from which each of us springs—that place with a certain lay of the land, with roads or walks, parents, grandparents, brothers, sisters, friends, voices, and smells, all deeply part of us; that place where we find our voices and animating passions. It is a home place.

Gender, race, socioeconomic status, sexual preference, culture, place—all contribute to social location. Everyone has a unique personal social location; however, hermeneutics emphasizes the social dimensions of the term, locations that express the experiences of social groups. For example, I came to college not only from a rural place in Minnesota geographically but with the rural mind-set and farm experience that many people I knew shared socially. I experienced my social location when a new faculty member from New York City laughed at a poem I wrote about listening to the corn grow, snapping and unwinding in late July sun. I wrote the poem from my social location as a farmer's daughter who had cultivated fifteen hundred acres of corn every summer from the time I was twelve. This was before Garrison Keillor made the soft, gravel roads of our everyday lives in Lake Wobegon nationally familiar as a social location on his *Prairie Home Companion* Sunday night radio show. Today my social location has shifted; I'm an urban professional. My original location, however, is one to which I can consciously return. I can talk weather, planting, haying, feeding hogs, and milking cows as well as the languages of my education—critical theory, narrative structures, and patriarchal social constructs. Feminist political theorist Iris Marion Young distinguishes an aggregate ("any classification of person according to some attribute," such as eye color) from a social group, which arises in people's experiences of the differences in their ways of life.

> A social group is a collective of persons differentiated from at least one other group by cultural forms, practices, or way of life. Members of a group have a specific affinity with one another because of their similar experience of way of life, which prompts them to associate with one another more than with those not identified with the group.[17]

Interestingly, people whose social locations are on the margins typically have double or triple vision; they know themselves through their difference from one or more dominant social groups. Women know male social location and experience their own as different. Jewish feminist Judith Plaskow explains that although "women's self-experience is an experience of selfhood, it is not women's experience that is enshrined in language or that has shaped our cultural forms.[18] Women must measure themselves against a standard that comes from outside their experience, for "the social and historical situation of the Other is not the same as the situation of one who take identity for granted."[19]

Another image of social location is that employed by social ethicist Toinette Eugene. After meditating on a painting of a two-headed phoenix rising, and recalling Alice Walker's essay entitled "Journal," which describes a two-headed woman, Eugene plays with images of two-headedness. One head dozes and the other speaks. Two-headed people are wise with more than one way of seeing but subject to extermination for their difference. Eugene argues for "an ethical biblical interpretation that is able to include as many people as there are disenfranchised," to hear suppressed voices.[20]

Drawing on her experience of double otherness as an African American and a woman, bell hooks defines her social location as a margin that is, first of all, a geographical place in her Kentucky hometown across the tracks where African Americans lived and, second, a margin between inside and outside.

> To be in the margin is to be part of the whole but outside the main body. As black Americans living in a small Kentucky town, the railroad tracks were a daily reminder of our marginality. Across those tracks were paved streets, stores we could not enter, restaurants we could not eat in, and people we could not look directly in the face. Across those tracks was a world we could work in as maids, as janitors, as prostitutes, as long as it was in a service capacity. We could enter that world but we could not live there. We had always to return to the margin, to cross the tracks to shacks and abandoned houses on the edge of town. There were laws to ensure our return. Not to return was to risk being punished. Living as we did—on the edge—we developed a particular way of seeing reality. We looked both from the outside in and from the inside out. We focused our attention on the center as well as on the margin. We understood both. This mode of seeing reminded us of the existence of a whole universe, a main body made up of both margin and center. Our survival depended on an ongoing public awareness of the separation of margin and center and an ongoing private acknowledgment that we were a necessary, vital part of that whole.[21]

Social location at the margin offers a view of the whole that differs from the view from the center; in fact, people at the center have little access to experience from different social location. They live unaware of others' differences from them. By naming and speaking experiences from the margins, women stand the ground of their presence in the whole. Bringing women and other "others" from the margin to the center of dialogue and conversation is a generative move, a recognition that experiences go unsaid or disclaimed because, without being named, they do not exist.

As an ethical method, a hermeneutic of liberation listens to the unheard voices of people who, like women, are marginalized, exploited, violated, invisible, or disempowered.[22] It privileges their critique of their oppressors, their view from the underside. The underside is not the home of victims but the homeplace of people who survive in the face of oppression. People who speak from the margins have their own stories of survival and solidarity to tell. Anna Julia Cooper calls this voice "a singing something." It is her image for speech from the unheard social location of an African American woman a century ago. The irrepressible voice in the human person echoes God's voice in the face of oppression; it is humankind's likeness to God for Cooper, as Karen Baker-Fletcher writes:

> It is in song, in voice, that humankind is created in the image of God, or better, in the sound of God. The entire body is engaged in voice. . . . Voice engages the whole person: the body, the mind, the feelings. Cooper's metaphor of a "Singing Something" points to the sacredness of human being as an energy and force that moves the body into action. Through voice one can assert the sacredness and beauty of Black women's bodies and lives.[23]

In her reflecting, bell hooks acknowledges that education has an homogenizing effect and that claiming one's homeplace as a site for resistant discourse must be a conscious act, if the same margins that are sites of oppression are to become social locations for generating new, resistant speech.

> I make a definite distinction between the marginality which is imposed by oppressive structures and that marginality one chooses as site of resistance—as location of radical openness and possibility. This site of resistance is continually formed in that segregated culture of opposition that is our critical response to domination. We come to this space through suffering and pain, through struggle. We know struggle to be that which pleasures, delights, and fulfills desire. We are transformed, individually, collectively, as we make radical creative space which affirms and sustains our subjectivity, which gives us a new location from which to articulate our sense of the world.[24]

To place her work in its context in the black community, womanist theologian Katie Cannon intentionally appends her own story to the essays in *Katie's Canon* and makes its purpose and social location clear in the title, "Exposing My Home Point of View."[25] Social location is a consciously examined and chosen homeplace, lived ground of survival, and seed ground of fully inclusive, democratic speech and community.

Rebecca Chopp understands the margins around the social-symbolic order as free space, where women whose experience the dominant order does not express can generate new discourse that corrects, changes, subverts, interrupts, and transforms the social-symbolic order.[26] The women disciples in Mark inhabit the textual location of the story's end; their silence as story characters sets up a dynamic interrelationship between said and unsaid, between what the text expresses and what hearers must interpret when they bring their lives into conversation with the narrative. In the silence of these characters who witness Jesus' death, burial, and proclaimed resurrection, the author trusts the narrative to claim people's lives and impel them to speak the proclamation. At the frontier edge of the written proclamation, the women's silence generates speech ahead of the narrative.

Feminist hermeneutics of liberation are incomplete without articulating ethics for generative, resistant speech in which women (and men) today can engage their truth (and illusion) with the truth (and illusion) of tradition. The rhetoric that silences the women disciples as story characters and suspends the narrative itself at 16:8b recognizes that the text creates and communicates truth claims for a receiver, who alone can conclude the text by wrestling from its fictional world an emancipatory word for her or his real world today and who alone can speak from her or his homeplace the reality in which she or he receives the word. The written Gospel communicates what Jesus and his disciples can no longer speak, a promise that must arrive and arise in the receivers of the word.

The textual location of the three women disciples at the empty tomb and at the boundary of the text makes Mark 16:8b an ideal site for generative feminist discourse. Their silence calls forth and privileges the voice of the hearer, the response of every person to the news that Jesus has gone ahead of his disciples as he promised. Susan Thistlethwaite in *Sex, Race, and God: Christian Feminism in Black and White* speaks for the necessity of privileging a diversity of voices in feminist discourse that creatively compensates for past silences, of which Mark 16:8 is one.

> What is called the natural world is always mediated by human consciousness and its social conditions. The social location of each woman is a primary constituent of her experience and is not directly accessible to the experience of women of other social locations.[27]

The biases and silences of the past cannot and need not be the norm of the future. The original ending of Mark resists putting words in hearers' mouths and calls instead for hearers to bring to language whatever reference the truth claims of the story have in their own experience and world. We humans have our being in words. The daring rhetorical silence that ends the Markan discourse resists all interpretation that does not include the hearer. This daring call fits well for men and women today educated for democratic citizenship. It makes our participation in interpreting the Gospel for our lives and world essential. Just as communicative justice demands that people have voice in decisions that affect them, so this principle insists that we have voice in meanings that identify and define us.[28]

Feminist hermeneutics of liberation calls readers to demanding practices in its work of widening the circle and multiplying the differences of those who speak the truth of their experience and seek to build the kin*dom of God among us. This study recognizes the following liberation hermeneutics as vital to its interpretation of Mark 16:8.

1. Privilege diversity. Invite others to speak for themselves.[29]

2. Listen others into speech. Attend to women's efforts to speak their experience.[30]

3. Name and speak one's own experience. Stand the ground of one's experience.[31]

4. Play in the space between the text and experience. Think abductively, that is, create new meanings, infer new possibilities, generate new song, liturgy, vision.[32]

5. Claim the promises of God toward the future. Testify to the activity of God in oneself and in the world.[33]

6. Be fully human—act reflectively, decide deliberately, understand intelligently, experience fully, interpret skillfully.[34]

7. Love, which means engaging in conversation with willingness to let one's mind be changed yet make one's own opinion, argument, and knowledge available, to persuade and be persuaded.[35] Put at risk all present self-understanding by facing the claims to attention of the other.[36]

Such feminist and liberation hermeneutics empower the community that receives the Gospels today to resist the biases against women in the texts and interpretative traditions and to perform the text as emancipatory proclamation toward constituting a Christian community of equals in our time.

To readers two millennia later, the Gospels are clearly the *first* Christians' word but not the *last* or *only* word. The Gospels carry the authority of the first communities in which they arose, but we today stand in a two-thousand-year tradition of their effects and the communities over time that they have constituted. A work that lasts provokes response. In lasting, a work may so transform the horizon of readers that it no longer provokes.[37] For example, the 1990 production of the musical *Hair*, performed for a generation of students born after the end of the Vietnam War, can no longer provoke action to end the war or burn draft cards. There is no war. No one has draft cards. The musical still embodies youthful disrespect, energy, and conflicts, but for a later generation it does not evoke civil disobedience. The first Gospel changes the horizon of its audience, creating a genre others imitated and used to new purposes. The New Testament does not tell us how Mary Magdalene, Mary the mother of James and Joses, and Salome lived out their lives as disciples as it does tell us about Peter and James. A telling of Jesus' story that excludes women from among his disciples alienates women today.

Mark's Gospel is a Christian literary classic, which has been used continuously to constitute Christian community. This study recognizes revelation in the historical Jesus and in the early Christian communities that gathered in his name, in the Gospels and other New Testament scriptures, in the communities of interpretation that have received the narrative, including present communities of resistance that want to free the text of oppressive biases. What we can know about the historical Jesus and originating Christian communities through the Gospel narrative remains probable, because of the distance of the text from the events and from the author. Nonetheless, the text embodies the testimony of early Christian communities and the Gospel writers about who Jesus is. As literature, the Gospel remains available through time to readers and hearers who can decode and respond to its truth claims.

Ultimately, the resistant reader shares in granting or not granting the narrative authority with the question, "Do its truth claims authorize my life, name my identity, stir me to trust God's promises, and take up Jesus' mission in our world?" The first Gospel is a narrative with a long history of being received and received again, of transforming its receivers and of their transforming its impact. The test of the Gospel's normative claims for the future rests in its continuing power to constitute justice-seeking, loving, and egalitarian Christian communities.

Women of Galilee

There stood looking on at a distance Mary Magdalene, Mary the mother of James and Joses, Salome, and many other women from Galilee who followed and served Jesus and had come up with him to Jerusalem. (Mark 15:40–41)

THESE TWO VERSES from near the end of the first Gospel introduce women who witness Jesus' death, burial, and proclaimed resurrection at the empty tomb. Mark's Gospel does not use the word "disciples" in describing them. Indeed, the first Gospel focuses predominantly on Jesus' male disciples and obscures the presence of women in their company.

Jesus calls five men by name to follow him—Peter, Andrew, James, and John in Mark 1:16–20 and Levi in Mark 2:14. Jesus invites twelve to a mountain and chooses them to be with him (3:13–19); the Gospel includes their names. The male disciples follow Jesus from this point on in the narrative until all except Peter scatter at Jesus' arrest (14:50). Frequently Jesus instructs them in private (4:10–11; 7:17–23; 8:17–21; 9:9–13, 31–32, 34–50; 10:23–45; 11:21–26; 13; 14:17–31, 37–38). Their presence pervades the narrative, while the women disciples remain invisible in the story until the end, when two verses reveal they have been with Jesus in Galilee and have come with him to Jerusalem. To counter this androcentric focus on the male disciples, feminist Bible scholars bring into the foreground for study the three words Mark uses to identify these women as disciples—"to follow" (*akolouthein*), "to serve" (*diakonein*), and "to come up with" (*synanabainein*).[1]

In Mark's Gospel the verb "to follow" means literally "to walk behind" Jesus in his lifetime, to leave one's own livelihood and go where Jesus goes, including making his journey to Jerusalem. It is a response to an invitation from Jesus. This physical, geographical journey also implies making a faith journey, learning from Jesus, hearing his teaching, seeing his healing actions, and ultimately recognizing his messianic identity. In fact, after Jesus, the disciples are the Gospel characters readers know most about. The first Gospel narrates their journey to faith as well as Jesus' journey through suffering and death to new life.

In Mark 1:17 Jesus, walking along the north shore of the Sea of Galilee, sees fishermen named Simon and Andrew and extends an invitation to them. "Come after me," Jesus says, and in response they "follow" (*ēkolouthēsan*) him. A little farther on, Jesus sees James and John and calls to them (1:20). The narrative reports they also "follow him." In 2:14, Jesus says to the tax collector Levi, "Follow me" (*Akolouthei moi*), and arising, Levi "follows him" (*ēkolouthēsen autǭ*). Two verses later the omniscient narrator makes the general statement that many followed Jesus (2:16). A second generalizing passage says that a great multitude from Judea, Jerusalem, Idumea, the region beyond the Jordan, Tyre, and Sidon "followed" him (3:7–8). A crowd "follows" Jesus as he goes with Jairus, who wants him to lay hands on his sick daughter (5:24). The narrative doesn't tell its readers how persistently individuals in the crowd follow; presumably the crowd has a looser commitment than the named individuals who follow Jesus throughout the narrative.

Indeed, Mark describes Jesus forming an inner circle of named male disciples. In Mark 3:14, Jesus goes up a mountain, calls those he wishes to him, and names twelve to be "with him" (*met' autou*). The special setting, choosing, and naming single out this group, the same in number as the twelve sons of the patriarch Jacob, from whom the tribes and people of Israel descend. This number suggests that Jesus is gathering together the beginnings of a new Israel. Jesus sends them out to preach, heal, and cast out demons—the same work he does (3:14–15). Jesus also sends the twelve out in 6:7. When they return (6:30), the narrative calls them "ones sent" (*apostoloi*). This verse and 3:14 are the only places in Mark's Gospel in which this term is used. As Jesus takes these *apostoloi* to a desert place, people recognize him and soon a crowd gathers; he begins to teach the crowd because they seem like "sheep without a shepherd" (6:34), that is, people without anyone to follow. Roman Catholic tradition interprets

Jesus' choosing twelve male disciples and sending them out as a precedent for limiting its priesthood to males.

In 8:31, halfway though Mark's Gospel, Jesus turns toward Jerusalem and prophesies for the first of three times that "the Son of Man will suffer many things, be rejected by the elders, chief priests, and scribes, and be killed, and after three days rise again." Jesus repeats this prediction twice more as he and his disciples walk from Galilee to Jerusalem (Mark 8:31–10:52). Within this journey section of the narrative, which features the three predictions that anticipate the final events of Jesus' life, the implied author also tucks sayings that define following Jesus more generically to include later generations of disciples, who, although they cannot literally walk to the cross with Jesus can nonetheless follow him. "If any want to become my followers, let them deny themselves and take up their cross and follow me" (*akoloutheitō moi*, 8:34).

On the journey to Jerusalem, Jesus invites new people to follow him. Jesus calls a rich young man to sell his possessions, give the money to the poor, and then follow him and take up the cross. This is a level of discipleship to which the young man cannot commit but to which those disciples on the journey have committed, a company that includes women as well as men. As part of the discussion of how the rich can be saved, Peter remarks to Jesus, "we left all things and followed [*ēkolouthēkamen*] you" (10:28). Jesus promises that those who forsake house and family for the sake of him and the gospel will receive a hundredfold. These references to family echo Jesus' words when his mother and brothers come to seek him. "Whoever does the will of God is my brother, sister, and mother" (3:35). The will of God evolves in the first Gospel beyond keeping the commandments, as the rich young man does, to following Jesus to the cross. Those who put their lives on the line for Jesus and the gospel, even if they lose their lives, will save them (8:35). To Peter's reminder in Mark 10:28 that he and the others have left all things, Jesus responds that those who leave house, brothers, sisters, father, mother, wife, or children, or fields for his sake and the gospel will receive in this age a hundredfold houses, brothers, sisters, mothers, children, and fields "with persecution." The implied author of Mark deliberately sets these sayings within Jesus' journey to Jerusalem with his first disciples, a section of Mark unified by Jesus' three prophecies that he will be handed over in Jerusalem, suffer, die, and be raised up on the third day. The journey takes place in the story, but the sayings extend the meaning of discipleship to later disciples who cannot literally walk behind Jesus to Jerusalem and the cross but whom Jesus calls to give their lives over to preaching and living the gospel. Conversely, those who are ashamed of Jesus, the Son of Man will be ashamed of when he comes in glory (8:38). The implied author has plotted that narrative to relate the journey of every disciple to the first disciples' paradigmatic journey with Jesus to the cross, a journey many women make with him.

James and John use the metaphor of drinking the cup to pledge their total commitment to following Jesus. When the two ask to sit at Jesus' right and left hand when he comes into his kingdom, Jesus asks, "Can you receive the baptism with which I will be baptized? Can you drink the cup I will drink?" They insist brashly, "We can," not anticipating they are pledging their lives, even to martyrdom.

In Mark 10:32 Jesus on the way to Jerusalem walks ahead of his disciples, who follow him amazed and afraid. Their fear prompts him to make his third and final prophecy of all that will happen in Jerusalem. At Jericho, the last stop on the way up to Jerusalem, a blind beggar named Bartimaeus, to whom Jesus gives sight, immediately follows Jesus on his way (10:52), exemplifying a wholehearted response that is the opposite of the rich young man's hesitation. In 14:28 Jesus again uses the image of shepherd and sheep when he tells his disciples they will all be scandalized. He quotes scripture: "I will strike the shepherd and the sheep will be scattered." Jesus goes on to promise that he will go before them to Galilee after his resurrection.

The foregoing analysis shows that at the story level of the Markan text "to follow" means literally following behind Jesus on his journey to Jerusalem, where religious and imperial authorities reside and where suffering and death await. This journey provides the plotted framework to which the author adds sayings to define discipleship for the Gospel's audience in 70 C.E. as taking up one's own cross and following Jesus, of losing one's life for the sake of Jesus and the gospel in order to save it, of drinking the cup of which Jesus drank. Only first-generation followers can be disciples in the literal sense of walking with or accompanying Jesus to Jerusalem. As the eyewitness characters make their journey in the narrative, Jesus' sayings address later disciples, for whom taking up the cross becomes a formative metaphor.

The women of Galilee are eyewitness characters who accompany Jesus to Jerusalem and, unlike all other disciples in the story, journey all the way to the cross. Luise Schottroff observes, "Mark sees the women under the cross as the representatives of the disciples and their carrying of the cross."[2] Although no women are among the twelve Jesus calls to be with him or among those he sends out to preach, heal, and cast out demons, still the narrative reveals that many women have followed Jesus in Galilee and come with him (*synanabasai*) (15:41) to Jerusalem. In its only other New Testament use, the verb "to come up with" (*synanabainein*) refers to disciples who are witnesses of the resurrection.

And for many days Jesus appeared to those who came up with him from Galilee to Jerusalem, who are now his witnesses to the people. (Acts 13:31)[3]

Diakoneō is also a word that connotes discipleship in Mark's Gospel. Besides describing the women at the cross in Mark 15:40, this word occurs only three times in Mark's Gospel. Angels "minister" (*diēkonoun*) to Jesus after Satan tempts him (1:13). Peter's mother-in-law "serves" (*diēkonei*) Jesus and the earliest disciples he calls to follow him—Peter, Andrew, James, and John (1:31). Jesus concludes the scene in which James and John ask for seats at his right and left in his glory with the saying that defines the meaning of serving in Mark's Gospel—"to give one's life" (Mark 10:45). In her research into the meaning of this verse, Luise Schottroff concludes that "usages of 'to serve' in the context of women's discipleship (Mark 1:31 and par.; Mark 15:41 and par) are to be understood as denoting discipleship and not hierarchical gender division of labor in which women do all the work of looking after other people's needs."[4]

Schottroff's research on women's place in early Christian social history finds evidence that free men served slaves and free women in domestic work and that early Christian communities struggled to practice the mutuality that service in Mark's Gospel and footwashing in John's Gospel express.[5] She insists that in the community of disciples the first Gospel addresses "all are servants of all. Service therefore has in Mark a much broader sense than table service: it describes the relation of the disciples with each other, the relations of disciples to Jesus, and also of Jesus to other people (10:45)."[6] Schottroff rightly sees *diakonia* as "an idea nearly synonymous with *akolouthein*" (to follow).[7] In her view it is the women's service of Jesus that takes them to his grave to anoint his body (Mark 16:1). The women of Galilee follow Jesus to the cross and serve him to the grave. The service (*diakonia*) of these women, mentioned in 15:41 and enacted in 16:1, echoes the actions of Peter's mother-in-law (1:29–31) and the anonymous woman's anointing of Jesus for burial (14:3–9). Thereby, women's acts of service frame both the whole Gospel and the passion story.

The verb *diakoneō* can mean taking care of physical needs, serving the table, and, according to Jesus' definition within the text, *giving one's life*. A feminist reading of the word *diēkonei* in the account of Peter's mother-in law transforms the narrative from a miracle story to the call of Jesus' first woman disciple. If one translates the word *diēkonei* in the story "she began to wait on them" (NAB), the reader sees Peter's mother-in-law making a little lunch for her son-in-law's new friends—a stereotypical domestic female role. Such translations, while valid, express no connotation of discipleship. However, Jesus specifically defines *diakonēsai* in Mark 10:45, equating serving with giving one's life, "For the Son of Man also came not to be served but *to serve* and *to give his life as a ransom for many*." A feminist reading of this three-verse cameo insists on applying Jesus' definition to translating the verb *diēkonei*. This is her story as the New Revised Standard Version tells it. It takes place on the first Sabbath of Jesus' ministry.

> As soon as they left the synagogue, they entered the house of Peter and Andrew, with James and John. Now Simon's mother-in-law was in bed with a fever, and they told him about her at once. He came and took her by the hand and lifted her up. Then the fever left her, and she began to serve them. (Mark 1:29–31)

In Mark 1:31 Jesus raises up (*ēgeiren*) Peter's mother-in-law, an implicit call, and she serves him and his male disciples (*diēkonei autois*). In response to his raising her up, she gives her life to serving Jesus in his new community. She becomes a disciple. In this story Jesus and his new male disciples come to be served; the woman is the exemplary disciple in the scene, the one who serves. Monika Fander recognizes that Peter's mother-in law is the exemplary disciple on the first Sabbath (Mark 1:21–34), which begins the representative first days of Jesus' ministry:

> Within the composition of the representative first days of Jesus' work, the problem of following is illustrated through the model reaction of a woman to whom not only the miracle-besotted multitudes but also the disciples stand in contrast. Through the insertion of the disciples' names in 1:29, the story becomes a discipleship story, in which a woman is represented not only for the reader but also for the first-called as a model follower and true disciple.[8]

The word *serve* in the three verses about Peter's mother-in-law makes a key link with the two verses about the women of Galilee in Mark 15:40–41 near the end of the narrative. Her story places women among Jesus' disciples from the beginning in Galilee. The word Mark uses to describe how Jesus raises her up (*ēgeiren*) is the same word he uses to speak of resurrection from the dead (12:26) and Jesus' own resurrection (14:28; 16:6), so her story resonates with the empty tomb story. Mark's Gospel repeatedly uses the word *egeirein* to describe Jesus' action in healing miracles. He commands the paralyzed man whose sins he has forgiven, "Arise (*egeire*) take up your mat and walk" (2:9, 11). He commands the man with the withered hand to "arise" (*egeire)* in the midst of the synagogue (3:3). He commands Jairus's daughter, whom all perceive to be dead, "Arise" (*egeire*) (5:41). Jesus takes the epileptic boy by the hand and "raises him" (*ēgeiren auton*, 9:27), just as he did Peter's mother-in-law. People around blind Bartimaeus direct him: "arise (*egeire)*, he calls you" (10:49). The repeated word choice and the gesture of raising people up relate these healings to Jesus' own being raised up from death. Both Jairus's daughter and the epileptic boy appear dead when Jesus raises them up, making the likeness and prelude to his resurrection more explicit.

The implied author of Mark weaves the cameo about Peter's mother-in-law among other story scenes near the beginning of the narrative. Jesus heals her on the Sabbath but in private at home. In Mark 3:1–6 Jesus heals a man's shriveled hand on the Sabbath at the synagogue. The Sabbath setting of both stories in effect makes Peter's mother-in-law also one for whom the Sabbath is made (2:28). Her private healing on the Sabbath is imperceptible in the Markan plot without a feminist hermeneutics that calls for bringing women in the text from the margin to the center of interpretation.

Peter's mother-in-law establishes an intergenerational context early in the Gospel. The later story of Jesus' mother and brothers coming to him (3:31–35) echoes Mark 1:29–31, when Jesus, his disciples, and Peter's mother-in-law implicitly form a new community. In the later scene Jesus raises the question, "Who are my mother and brothers?" He repudiates the blood relationship between mother and son as constitutive of his family and identifies the uniting bond to be the shared commitment to doing the will of God—"Whoever does the will of God is my brother and sister and mother" (3:35). Fidelity and obedience to God are the relationships that bind together the community of his followers with Jesus. By this criterion, Peter's mother-in-law belongs to the community he is gathering. The saying in Mark 3:35 also explicitly mentions "sister" (*adelphē*) among those who do the will of God and belong to this family that is related by faith rather than blood.

The women of Galilee who follow and serve Jesus (15:40–41) are not Jesus' first women disciples in the narrative. Peter's mother-in-law is. She is, like them, a woman of Galilee whom the Gospel pictures serving Jesus, giving her life to the new community (1:29–31). Her presence shows women to be among Jesus' closest disciples from the beginning of his ministry; the women at the cross and tomb show that women were among his disciples beyond its end. Jesus' saying that those who do the will of God are brother, sister, and mother to him confirms the presence of women among his followers.

The proper anointing of Jesus' body, which Mary Magdalene, Mary the mother of James and Joses, and Salome set out to do at dawn on the first day of the week (16:1–2), echoes the anointing that takes place just before Jesus' passion, an anointing that Jesus says must be told in the woman's memory wherever the gospel is proclaimed (14:9). This saying, which concludes the story, makes this unnamed woman's anointing of Jesus' head with expensive ointment (14:3–9) an integral part of the good news, as integral as the women's discovery of the empty tomb. The anointing in 14:3 anticipates the necessity of anointing Jesus' body for burial, a purpose Jesus recognizes in 14:8. The anonymous woman anoints Jesus before he is dead; the women of Galilee who seek to anoint his dead body find his tomb empty and cannot complete their task. The anonymous woman's anointing supposedly for death proves a prophetic anointing of Jesus as messiah, the identity his resurrection confirms. These two anointing stories have an inverse relationship—the first completes before the fact of Jesus' death an anointing that proves impossible in the second scene. The impossibility of accomplishing this second anointing and the good news that Jesus is risen put the first anointing in a new light; this anointing on the head prophetically discloses that the one who was crucified is indeed the messiah.

Jesus praises the woman's lavish action, but other disciples object. Unlike these others eating at Simon the Leper's house with Jesus, this unnamed woman accepts Jesus' impending death and acclaims his messianic identity. Jesus praises her for doing what she can for him. The scene ends with Jesus insisting that her action be told in her memory wherever the good news is proclaimed throughout the world. Small wonder her action should be proclaimed; it summarizes the good news. Her prophetic action foreshadows Jesus' climactic affirmation "I am" to the high priest's question, "Are you the messiah, the Son of the Blessed One?" Her prophetic action reaches to the end of the story, where Jesus, whom she anointed as king, does not need to be anointed for death, because he is no longer in the tomb. Proclaiming this woman's action proclaims Jesus' messianic identity—the good news. The woman herself is silent and nameless in the story, but her action interprets the whole of Jesus' death and resurrection. The anointing proves to be for kingship not death.

In sum, stories of women who follow and serve Jesus and belong to his company of disciples frame the whole Gospel narrative and the passion narrative. Their stories claim such minimal space in the narrative that their presence remains invisible without a feminist perspective to maximize their importance. The actions of the women who follow, serve, and anoint Jesus are not trivial but representative of exemplary discipleship. The text represents their presence with Jesus minimally yet distinctively and integrally to the full characterization of discipleship. Peter and all the male disciples with Jesus at the Passover supper insist they will die with Jesus rather than deny him (14:31). Their actions betray their confident words. All but Peter leave Jesus and flee at his arrest (14:50); Peter denies him three times (14:68, 70, 71). The story expresses the women's discipleship in action. They follow farther than all others in the narrative. They witness the crucifixion. They see where Jesus is buried. They take on the work of rolling back the gravestone and giving Jesus' body a proper anointing. Like the woman Jesus praises for anointing him for burial (14:6, 8), the Galilean women do what they can. Their service is elemental. They stand with someone they love to the end and help bury his body.

CHAPTER 6

Numinous Fear

❦

Because they were afraid. (Mark 16:8)

MARK NOT ONLY TELLS JESUS' STORY in the first Gospel but characterizes Jesus' disciples in moments of numinous awe that invite hearers of the story to recognize their own fear as the threshold of faith in Jesus. Mark is a narrative theologian who arranges plot, characters, and setting to communicate who Jesus is and to invite hearers to faith in him.

The final words of the original ending of the first Gospel, "And they said nothing to anyone because they were afraid," characterize the three women who have followed and served Jesus from Galilee to Jerusalem, who do not fear witnessing his crucifixion, who do not fear burying his dead body, and who do not fear opening a closed tomb, suddenly struck dumb by paralyzing fear. Until this last verse, when the women flee the tomb trembling and beside themselves and say nothing to anyone about finding it empty or about hearing the good news that Jesus is risen from a young man inside, until then Mary Magdalene, Mary the mother of James and Joses, and Salome are the most exemplary and faithful disciples in the narrative. A contrast so stark and abrupt can only represent an author's deliberate rhetorical strategy, although many scholars interpret this fear not as numinous awe inviting reader response but as the utter failure of Jesus' last faithful disciples.[1]

The final verse of Mark contains three words in Greek for fear—*tromos, ekstasis,* and *ephobounto.*

And they went out and fled from the tomb; for *trembling* (*tromos*) and *astonishment* (*ekstasis*) had come upon them; and they said nothing to anyone, for they were *afraid* (*ephobounto*). (16:8)

The women's fear is one of twelve references to fear in Mark's Gospel, indicating that this emotion is an important recurring characterization. In examining these references, Andrew T. Lincoln refuses to interpret the women's fear in 16:8 as "just stunned silence before the transcendent" or a narrative means for the women to defer to the male disciples. This fear is negative, inciting silence, flight, and failure.[2] Mary Ann Tolbert reads the first Gospel ironically as a story of failed discipleship.[3] On the other hand, J. Lee Magness examines the fear and silence in which Mark's Gospel ends within the structure of reactions to the miraculous throughout the Gospel. The women's fear in Mark 16:8 is fear on a new level— a heightened, numinous fear; their silence, a trigger for the reader to remember the proclamation made in the beginning and many times throughout the text—Jesus is the Christ, the Son of God (1:1).[4]

None of these scholars explores the story scenes about fear within the chiasmic literary patterns the implied author arranges in the narrative to lead the hearer/reader and to make one story comment theologically on another. Mark's narrative is not a linear string of individual anecdotes, a string of pearls; rather its composition is circular with patterns of echoes and oral paragraphing that reflect the proximity of its oral past. A literary reading of Mark identifies fear as an existential threshold of faith not only in the last verse but in earlier narrative sections as well.

Mark's Gospel has three sets of double stories: twice Jesus' disciples cross the Sea of Galilee in bad weather (4:35–41; 6:45–52); twice Jesus feeds multitudes of people with a few loaves and fishes (6:34–44; 8:1–10); twice Jesus heals blind men (8:22–26; 10:46–52).[5] These doublets create frames in the narrative, oral parentheses that signal hearers when thematic sections of the narrative begin and end. The doublets help structure listening and reading, alerting hearers and readers to consider how the stories in between interplay on a theme.

In addition to doublets, the implied author of Mark repeatedly intercalates or intercuts one story within another, creating Markan sandwiches. For example, the story of the woman with a hemorrhage (Mark 5:24–34) interrupts the story of Jairus's daughter, which begins in 5:21–24 and continues in 5:35–43. The Jairus story is like two pieces of bread around a filling—the story of the woman with the hemorrhage. As in a sandwich, what is in the middle gives the whole its flavor. Intercalations signal the hearer to use the center story to interpret the outer story. Inter-calations, of which John R. Donahue lists seven instances in Mark, create a circular pattern; the end of the story takes up the beginning. One story wraps another.[6]

Five of the twelve times story characters experience fear in Mark's narrative (4:40–41; 5:15; 5:33–34; 5:36; 6:50–52) occur in verses that fall between the two stories about Jesus' disciples crossing the Sea of Galilee (4:35–41; 6:45–52). Three of the twelve instances of fear (9:6; 9:32; 10:32) occur on the journey to Jerusalem, a section framed by stories in which Jesus heals blind men (8:22–26; 10:46–52). These two long narrative sections are the first and third sections in a narrative chain that extends from 4:35 to 10:52. Two feedings miracles (6:34–44; 8:1–10) form the remaining doublet. The implicit author places the first feeding miracle just before the second sea-crossing story to interlock the first and second doublets. Twelve verses, 8:11–21, follow the second feeding miracle, a continuing reflection on the meaning of the miracles in which Jesus questions his disciples about the leaven of the Pharisees and their understanding of the twelve and seven baskets of leftovers. Figure 2 below diagrams how the three sets of doublets link across Mark's narrative.

Figure 2

A 4:35–41 Jesus calms the Sea of Galilee for his disciples, who are crossing in a boat and fear for their lives.

B 6:34–44 Jesus feeds 5,000 on the Galilee side of the lake.

A 6:45–52 Jesus calms wind on the Sea of Galilee for his disciples trying to row across.

B 8:1–10 Jesus feeds 4,000 on the other side of the lake.

C 8:22–26 Jesus heals blind man in two stages.

C 10:46–52 Jesus heals blind Bartimaeus in Jericho.

The stories between the two sea crossings contain two intercalations—the testimony of the woman healed of a hemorrhage happens within the story of Jesus' raising Jairus's daughter; the beheading of John the Baptist happens between Jesus' sending out his disciples to preach, expel demons, and heal the sick and their returning. The sea-crossing doublets and two intercalations give 4:35–6:52 a chiastic composition that directs hearers to use the stories at the centers of the intercalations to interpret the whole.

A chiasm, or chiasmus, takes its name from the Greek letter *chi*, written as an X, which is the same on the bottom and the top but inverted. Technical language can make a literary pattern seem complex and contrived when in fact chiasms are familiar in children's stories and well within a first grader's ability to narrate, as Danny Scorpio demonstrates in this adventure.

> Once upon a time I was in my house watching TV and I wanted to go on an adventure. So I turned off the TV and I got on my horse named Fred and went up the sidewalk and down the sidewalk to Caribou Coffee for a drink of cocoa. Then we went to my friend's house to play. The horse had to stay outside while we played. When I came outside again we rode to my Grandma's house. Of course the horse had to stay outside. Then we rode to my mom's office. The horse named Fred had to stay in the parking lot. After that we went to a cave. We looked in. A dragon named Pete was in there. Good thing I had my sword! The dragon named Pete woke up. He yelled at us. Then my horse named Fred ran past my Grandma's house, past my friend's house, past Caribou Coffee, up the sidewalk and down the sidewalk all the way home. The end.

The key action or turning point takes place at the center of a chiasm. The pattern unwinds the plot in reverse order from this center.

Figure 3 below outlines the chiastic structure of Mark 4:35–6:52, in which five of the twelve mentions of fear in Mark appear. In this chiasm, the last story repeats the themes of the first—A has an echo in A'. The second story (B) and the second to the last story repeat or relate in theme—B has an echo in B'. The third story (C) in the chiasm is the first half of the Jairus narrative, which resumes C' after the testimony of the woman with the hemorrhage (D). Her story is the turning point in the first intercalation, its interpretative key, the meat of the first Markan sandwich that helps form this chiasm. The beheading of John the Baptist (F) is the center of the second intercalation in the chiasm, the meat of the second Markan sandwich, which stands between the sending out (E) and the returning (E') of the disciples on mission. Jesus' prophetic precursor, John the Baptist, whose martyrdom expresses good reason for disciples to feel fear, and a nameless woman who tells a crowd the whole truth of her healing despite her fears are the key figures in this chiastic narrative pattern (fig. 3).

Figure 3

A 4:35–41 Jesus calms the storm on the Sea of Galilee that threatens to swamp the boat carrying him and his disciples to the Gentile side of the lake. Jesus chides the disciples for their fear and lack of faith. They ask, "Who is this whom the wind and sea obey?"

> **B 5:1–20** Jesus expels a legion of demons from a man who lives in chains among tombs in Gentile Gerasene territory. The Gerasenes react with fear and ask Jesus to leave.

>> **C 5:21–24** Jesus crosses the lake to the Jewish side; Jairus, a synagogue official, seeks out Jesus to heal his daughter, who lies ill at home.

>>> **D 5:24–34** A woman who has hemorrhaged for twelve years touches Jesus' cloak and is healed. He feels power go out and demands to know who touched him. The woman is afraid but speaks the whole truth of her healing.

>> **C' 5:35–43** Jesus raises Jairus's daughter from apparent death.

> **B' 6:1–6** Jesus preaches in Nazareth but people reject him in his hometown. He can work no miracles among the Nazarenes.

>> **E 6:7–13** Jesus sends disciples out two by two to preach repentance, expel demons, cure the sick.

>>> **F 6:14–29** Herod beheads John the Baptist.

>> **E' 6:30–33** Jesus' disciples return from mission.

A' 6:45–52 The disciples are rowing against the wind. Jesus comes walking on the water, tells them not to fear, gets in the boat, and the wind dies down.

Exploring in detail the kinds of fear in this chiasm shows Mark the theologian constructing a literary pattern to help readers and hearers recognize how faith begins. In the first crossing story (4:35–41), a storm comes up on the Sea of Galilee and waves fill the boat. Jesus' disciples fear for their lives and awaken Jesus, who rebukes the wind, calms the storm, and asks them why they are so fearful and have no faith. Jesus' actions and questions heighten the disciples' fear, "they were filled with a great awe" (*kai ephobēthēsan phobon megan*) (4:41). In their heightened fear or awe they ask a question that goes unanswered in the composition through 8:29, "Who then is this, that even the wind and the sea obey him?" During the second crossing story two chapters later, Jesus is praying on a mountain that overlooks the sea. The discourse gives Jesus an omnipotent presence, of which the disciples who are rowing across the lake against the wind are ignorant. When Jesus comes walking on the water past them, his disciples think he is a ghost. This sight troubles them. Jesus says, "It is I. Do not be afraid" (6:50). Although Jesus' presence should eliminate the disciples' fear, their reaction does not move to faith but remains a heightened fear or awe: "And they were utterly astounded within them" (6:51). At the beginning and end of this chiasm, the same characters—Jesus' first disciples—remain fearful. Jesus' absence endangers his men disciples and reveals their lack of faith; his presence brings them to numinous fear and amazed awe—a liminal threshold they do not cross. The narrative suspends them in fear heightened to awe.

In each of the A, B, and C stories that build toward the center of the chiasm, death threatens and gives characters reason for fear. The stormy sea is a potential tomb. The man possessed by a legion of demons lives among the tombs and has no life in the company of others. Illness threatens Jairus's daughter with death. At the center of the second intercalation is the story of John the Baptist's beheading. In the storm story, the disciples' fear that they will drown changes to a numinous fear in response to Jesus' calming of the waves. In the exorcism, the crowd from the Gerasene area responds to Jesus' power over demons with fear and rejects him, asking him to leave their territory. The woman with the hemorrhage experiences fear and trembling (*phobētheisa kai tremousa*) when Jesus wants to know who touched him. However, unlike the disciples in the boat or the people who witness the exorcism of the demoniac, she steps beyond her fear to speak her faith. Her fear proves a threshold to her faith. Her story in the eye of the intercalation and at the center of the larger chiasm models the step beyond fear to faith that Mark wants readers and hearers of the Gospel to take. The woman knows what has happened to her, falls down before Jesus, and tells him all the truth of her healing. She speaks her experience, testifies in the midst of the crowd about what has happened within her, where her life blood has been hemorrhaging. Jesus acknowledges her faith and says her faith has healed her, "Daughter, your faith has made you well" (5:34). The narrative cuts immediately to the news that Jairus's daughter has died, taking up with intensity the story the intercalation interrupts. Jesus advises Jairus, "Do not fear (*Mē phobou*), only believe." In this statement Jesus calls Jairus specifically to faith that Jesus can raise the dead girl to life. The intercalation shows that faith in Jesus heals and gives life. Jairus, Peter, James, and John experience numinous fear or amazement when the little girl gets up and walks about (5:42). They are "overcome with amazement" (*exestēsan ekstasei megalē*). In the chiasm only the woman experiences such fear and crosses its threshold to actively giving witness to her faith. The named men disciples say nothing.

The chiastic structure places the rejection of the Gentile Gerasenes (B) and the rejection Jesus experiences from his hometown Nazarenes (B') as parallel echoing stories. In 5:1–20 Jesus is in Gentile territory: the people fear him and ask him to leave. In 6:1–6, Jesus is in Jewish territory in his hometown synagogue, where the people are so sure they know who he is that they cannot believe he is a prophet. They too reject him. The composition makes both the Gerasene crowd and the people in the Nazareth synagogue reject Jesus. The Gerasenes experience fear but close the door on the threshold it opens. The Nazarenes don't even experience fear; Jesus is not a prophet to them.

As figure 4 below summarizes, the first chiasma with its five mentions of fear spotlights the hemorrhaging woman's shift from fear to faith at its center (D). Jairus moves from concern that his daughter will die (C) to great amazement at her raising (C'). Both the Gerasenes (B) and the Nazarenes (B') reject Jesus—the Gerasenes out of fear and the Nazarenes out of unbelief. In the sea-crossing stories (A, A'), the composition describes the disciples in heightened, numinous fear. Characters' fear becomes numinous when they recognize signs of Jesus' divinity or actions of divine power.

The second intercalation within the sea-crossing doublet (fig. 4: E, F, E') wraps Jesus' sending of his twelve disciples out to preach, expel demons, and heal the sick—the very activities for which Gerasene and Nazareth crowds have rejected him—around the story of John the Baptist's beheading. This mission intercalation makes clear that Jesus' disciples can expect rejection and persecution if they do Jesus' work or continue the preaching of John the Baptist. Yet, in the whole narrative section which the sea-crossing stories frame, the narrative moves only the woman with the hemorrhage beyond numinous fear and trembling to faith and testimony and makes her example in the eye of the first intercalation the key to the interpretation of the whole. She models the faith and witness to which the discourse wants to persuade its hearers. She is a woman Jesus calls daughter, who has been healed of twelve years of bleeding that made her an unclean outsider among her coreligionists. Her identity as a daughter of Jesus suggests a similar future for the other daughter in the story, a twelve-year-old at the onset of menstruation, who lives because her father brings Jesus to her.

Figure 4

A 4:35–41 Disciples shift from fear for their lives to numinous fear or awe.

> **B 5:1–20** Gerasenes respond to Jesus' freeing the demoniac with numinous fear but ask him to leave.

> > **C 5:21–24** Jairus fears his daughter will die.

> > > **D 5:24–34** The woman experiences trembling and numinous fear because she knows what has happened to her. She speaks the whole truth. Her faith heals her.

> > **C' 5:35–43** Jesus tells Jairus not to fear, only believe. He responds to Jesus' raising his daughter up with great amazement.

> **B' 6:1–6** The people of Nazareth do not fear Jesus; they are sure they know him and reject his teaching. Jesus marvels at their unbelief.

A' 6:45–52 The disciples shift from feeling troubled by Jesus' appearance to amazement and wonder after he tells them not to fear and calms the wind.

Mission is an important theme in this section. Jesus sends the demoniac to preach to his own people (fig. 4: B). Jesus sends his disciples (fig. 4: E to E') to preach, heal, and cast out demons just as he has done (fig. 4: B, C, D, C', B'). The intercalation (E, F, E') wraps the mission of Jesus' disciples around the mission of John the Baptist, projecting the historical progression:

1. John the Baptist, the precursor

2. Jesus

3. Jesus' disciples

The first intercalation also suggests a time line; in it Jesus teaches, heals, and casts out demons, and two anonymous suppliants become witnesses of his work in their lives—the woman with the hemorrhage and the Gerasene demoniac. The narrative deliberately brings Peter, James, and John into the Jairus narrative but in a silent role. They are not the characters in the narrative who model discipleship and whose faith proclaims Jesus' healing and life-giving power. The anonymous suppliants' active testimony extends the time line to include two later generations of Jesus' disciples to follow those Jesus sends out, namely, the two healed but

anonymous suppliants who spread the good news of Jesus' healing and
life-giving power, and implicitly the twelve-year-old Jesus raises up to a
future different from the hemorrhaging woman's. This suggests the following historical progression in mission:

1. John the Baptist

2. Jesus

3. Jesus' disciples

4. Healed suppliants (demoniac, woman healed of hemorrhage)

5. Twelve-year-old daughter who is raised up

The framing doublets (A, A') picture Jesus' disciples at sea in the ambiguity between faith and fear, between the calm Jesus' presence with them
brings and the high and adverse winds of his absence. Life and death, Jew
and Gentile, fear and faith are oppositions woven into relation by this chiasm. The sea and the tombs are liminal places. The woman in the eye of
the first intercalation crosses over from fear to faith; John the Baptist in
the eye of the second intercalation has crossed from life to death. John's
fate gives Jesus and his followers good reason for fear. The decision to follow and believe in Jesus is a life-and-death matter. Faith heals in the first
intercalation, but mission endangers in the second. Faith in Jesus' power
to raise the dead girl to life is the key to all that threatens death—nature,
demons, illness; faith in Jesus' power to give life offers Jairus's daughter,
only twelve, a future.

The faith of the women in Mark 16:8b is most like the numinous fear
of the men disciples or the heightened amazement of Jairus. The narrative deliberately suspends Jesus' best-known, earliest women and men
disciples in numinous fear.

The Markan composition shows the disciples reacting with fear three
more times in the part of the composition framed by the doublets in
which Jesus heals blind men (8:22–10:52). Jesus' three passion predictions structure this section. Like three stepping stones, they advance the
story toward Jerusalem. To each of these predictions Jesus' disciples react
with fear and the narrative suspends them in this heightened, numinous
state. Peter, James, and John are the disciples who experience fear the first
time. They see Jesus transfigured in glory (Mark 9:2–10). They feel fearful (*ēsan gar ekphoboi*) and Peter does not know what to say (9:6). The
divine voice in this story answers the same question Jesus made his disciples answer just verses earlier in 8:27–30, when he asked, "Who do you

say that I am?" Then Peter enthusiastically answered, "The messiah." That is before Jesus makes his first passion prediction over Peter's protective objections. After this first prediction of his passion, Jesus takes Peter, James, and John to a mountaintop, where they see him transfigured in glory with two of Israel's greatest prophets, Moses and Elijah, who experienced people's rejection in their times (1 Kings 19:2–3, 10; Exodus 32:23) and were both expected to return (Malachi 4:5–6; Deuteronomy 18:15). The scene lifts Jesus' three best-known disciples into a numinous vision in which glory and rejection mix and confuse them. The voice from heaven addresses them and the reader, "This is my Son, the Beloved; listen to him."

Twice more the narrative suspends Jesus' disciples in fear. When Jesus predicts his passion a second time, they do not understand his words but are afraid to question him (9:32). At the time of the third prediction, the disciples, including the women, are on the way to Jerusalem with Jesus walking in their lead like a shepherd. The narrative says, "They were astonished, and although following after Jesus, afraid" (10:32). This third prediction scene suggests the same shepherd imagery Jesus uses in 14:27, when he predicts that the shepherd will be struck and the sheep will scatter but promises to go before them again, this time back to Galilee when he rises from the dead (14:28).

Deliberately in Mark 4:41; 6:52; 9:6, 32; and 10:32 the narrative suspends Jesus' first disciples in numinous fear much the way Mark 16:8b suspends the women disciples. The disciples' fear has a direct relation to their mission of continuing Jesus' work as Jesus continued the work begun by Israel's prophets from Moses through John the Baptist. Two anonymous suppliants believe and preach, the freed Gerasene and the newly whole woman. She is a model of moving through fear to faith and witness.

CHAPTER 7

Silence, Secrets, and Speech

☙

They said nothing to anyone. (Mark 16:8)

A LITERARY-CRITICAL APPROACH to Mark's Gospel assumes, as J. Lee Magness says well that "no part of a literary work is independent of the rest of the work."[1] Assuming that the women's silence in Mark 16:8b stands in literary and rhetorical coherence with the whole text, the interpreter can decode the implied author's use of silence as a literary motif and repeated rhetorical strategy and recognize what the narrative sets the audience up to hear when the women "say nothing to anyone." These words that frustratingly narrate silence at the very point plotted in the narrative for full revelation and proclamation, echo Jesus' command to the leper he heals in Mark 1:44, "Tell no one anything about this." The leper is not supposed to tell but does; the women should tell but do not. The command to the leper is the first of eight instances in which Jesus silences demons or enjoins healed suppliants and disciples not to tell who he is (1:25; 1:34; 1:44; 3:12; 5:43; 7:36; 8:30; 9:9), a literary motif widely termed among scholars the "messianic secret."

Three places in the story describe Jesus silencing demons because they know who he is. The first silencing happens on the first day of Jesus' ministry when he preaches at the Capernaum synagogue with newly called disciples Peter, Andrew, James, and John in attendance (1:21–28). When a man with an unclean spirit enters the synagogue, the unclean spirit recognizes who Jesus is and cries out, "What do you have to do with us,

Jesus of Nazareth? Have you come to destroy us? I know who you are, the Holy One of God" (1:24). The questions the unclean spirit voices are rhetorical questions that Jesus answers in action rather than words as he silences the spirit and frees the man. The synagogue worshipers see what Jesus does and raise questions of their own about his authority, "What is this? A new teaching with authority! He commands even the unclean spirits and they obey him" (1:27). The unclean spirit identifies Jesus as "the Holy One of God," letting readers and hearers of the narrative know what the Sabbath worshipers in the story do not realize about Jesus from his action. Jesus' fame, not his messianic identity, spreads in the narrative as a result of this incident. Through the voice of the unclean spirit, the narrative repeats the same christological claim that the superscription declares in Mark 1:1 and that the voice from heaven at Jesus' baptism confirms in 1:11.

Both Mark 1:32–34 and 3:7–12 expand the scenes in which Jesus heals individuals or frees them of demons to explain that he is healing and freeing all kinds of people in many villages. These generalizing scenes reiterate that Jesus will not permit the demons he expels to speak and reveal who he is. When scribes and Pharisees in Mark 3:22–27 suggest that Jesus has power over evil because he is evil, Jesus argues that Satan does not cast out Satan, a house does not divide against itself. By casting out demons, Jesus demonstrates the power of God. The demons function in the narrative to reveal to the reader that Jesus is the Son of God while concealing his identity from characters in the story.

In addition to these three passages, in which Jesus silences unclean spirits or demons, Jesus calls for silence in two related instances. When Jesus quiets the storm and wind on the Sea of Galilee (4:39), his power over nature raises a question of authority for his disciples, just as his casting out the demons in the Capernaum synagogue did for the worshipers there: "Who is this?" Indeed, who but God do the wind and storm obey?

Halfway through the narrative, when Peter objects to Jesus' first prediction of his passion, Jesus silences him and refers to him as Satan (8:33). Jesus silences Peter's unwillingness to recognize the teacher he has seen raise Jairus's daughter from the dead go to his own death. Both of these silencings in the story sharpen messianic claims that the narrative makes for the reader.

On three occasions Jesus requests secrecy of people he heals. In the first instance, the leper whom Jesus makes whole in Mark 1:40–45 and directs to "tell no one anything" nevertheless makes the story public. His proclamation of the good news of his healing brings sick people from all sides to Jesus hoping for a cure, which makes entering towns difficult for Jesus. In the second case, a healing story set in the Gentile Decapolis area (7:31–37), Jesus strictly enjoins both the man whose ears he opens and whose tongue he looses and the man's friends not to tell anyone. But the more Jesus says not to tell, the more this man and his friends proclaim what happened. Third, a little later at Bethsaida, Jesus commands the blind man whom he heals in two stages not to go into his village and not to tell anyone from the village about his sight and who gave it to him (8:22–26). The narrative does not disclose the suppliant's response. Two of three suppliants whom Jesus commands not to tell who he is proclaim their healings anyway. If the location of the healings indicates the nationalities of the suppliants, then the leper is a Galilean Jew and the deaf mute from the Decapolis area, a Gentile.

On three occasions Jesus requests secrecy of Peter, James, and John. On the first of these occasions, Jesus takes the three to witness the raising of Jairus's daughter. He enjoins them as well as Jairus and his wife not to tell anyone. "He enjoined them strictly not to let anyone know about it" (5:43). Indeed, in the Gospel narrative, these named disciples keep silent about this miracle just as the named women disciples keep silent about God's raising of Jesus from the dead.

On the second occasion, which begins in Mark 8:27, Jesus and his disciples journey to Caesarea Philippi, and for seven verses at this midpoint in the narrative discuss together who he is. A feminist perspective includes women in this group, since the text does not specifically exclude them. Jesus asks who people say that he is. The disciples report three possible identities—John the Baptist, Elijah, or one of the prophets. Then for the group Peter answers Jesus' question "Who do you say that I am?" with the confession "You are the messiah" (8:30). Jesus gives all the disciples with him "strict orders not to tell anyone about him." Again, the disciples keep the secret.

The transfiguration is the third occasion Jesus orders Peter, James, and John to be silent. As Jesus leads Peter, James, and John down the mountain after they have seen him in transfigured glory, Jesus "ordered them to tell no one about what they had seen, until after the Son of Man had risen from the dead" (9:9). As characters in the Markan story, Jesus closest disciples keep the secret Jesus enjoins on them. The transfiguration is the point in the plot that sets up the day of Jesus' resurrection as the time to tell who he is.

The foregoing analysis shows that Jesus' named men and women disciples are the story characters who keep the secret of his identity. Indeed, the messianic secret motif points to the same pattern that the fear motif shows. Numinous fear characterizes the named women disciples in 16:8b and the named men disciples in 4:41 and 6:52; silence characterizes the women in 16:8b and the men in 5:43, 8:30, and 9:9. The demons, Jairus and his wife, the unnamed blind man, and Jesus' best-known disciples all keep the secret of Jesus' power. The leper and deaf mute spread the good news that Jesus healed them, as does the Gerasene demoniac (5:20). Because the audience hears the story from the omniscient narrator's point of view, they, like the narrator, know who keeps the secret, who tells the secret, and what the secret is—Jesus is God's Son, the messiah, the strong one who has come to plunder Satan's house and has power over wind and storm, sickness and death. The narrative sets its audience up to hear the secret of Jesus' messianic identity from other voices than the named men or women disciples.

Five times the narrative raises significant questions about who Jesus is. In the first two instances the questions are rhetorical, leaving them for hearers' response. The other three have simple, direct answers which make christological confessions. The questions arch christological claims across the narrative, claims that Donald Juel sees forming the substructure of New Testament Christianity.

> The confession of Jesus as the crucified and risen King of the Jews stands at the beginning of Christological reflections and interpretation of the scriptures—at least the reflection and interpretation that form the substructure of New Testament Christianity.[2]

When Jesus calms the storm (Mark 4:41), his disciples exclaim, "Who is this that even the sea and wind obey him?" The disciples raise this question in awe of Jesus' power. As a rhetorical strategy, the discourse leaves this question unanswered, making its answer a commanding theme across the narrative. Of course, the implied answer is surely the Son of God, the Creator. The rhetorical questions that the people of Nazareth raise about Jesus' identity clearly reject any christological claims assigned to their hometown prophet. "Where did this man get all this? What is this wisdom that has been given to him? What deeds of power are being done by his hands? Is not this the carpenter, the son of Mary and brother of James and Joses and Judas and Simon, and are not his sisters here with us?" (6:2–3). In 8:27 and 29 Jesus himself raises the overarching question when he asks his disciples, "Who do people say that I am?" and "Who do you say that I am?" Peter answers, "You are the messiah." Peter's response to Jesus' first passion prediction in the verses that follow immediately shows that Peter has no adequate idea of Jesus as messiah. The high priest repeats the key overarching question when he asks Jesus directly in 14:61, "Are you the Son of the Blessed One?" Jesus answers, "I am." Pilate, too, raises the same question when he asks Jesus in 15:2, "Are you the king of the Jews." Jesus answers indirectly, "You say so," ironically confirming that Pilate speaks the truth. The answers to the repeated questions waste no words. Their brevity sharpens their focus. Jesus is the messiah, the Son of God. However, the author sprinkles the narrative with additional answers to these questions. The first verse of the narrative calls Jesus the Christ and Son of God; the centurion echoes these words as a response to Jesus' death on the cross, "Clearly this man was the Son of God" (15:39). At Jesus' baptism, a voice speaks from heaven, "You are my Son, the Beloved; with you I am well-pleased" (1:11). The voice from heaven speaks a second time in the narrative at the transfiguration scene and repeats the message it spoke at Jesus' baptism, "This is my Son, the beloved" (9:7). The demons make christological confession when they see Jesus: "You are the holy one of God" (1:24); "You are the Son of God" (3:11); "What have you to do with me, Jesus, Son of the Most High God?" (5:6).

Jesus' messianic identity is implicitly at issue in questions about his authority. The worshipers who witness Jesus cast out an unclean spirit from a man in the Capernaum synagogue ask amazed, "What is this? A new teaching—with authority! He commands even the unclean spirits and they obey him" (1:27). Pharisees and scribes challenge his willingness to forgive a paralyzed man's sins rather than heal him—"Who can forgive sins but God?" (2:7). The chief priests, scribes, and elders raise these questions of authority in 11:28 when Jesus is teaching in the temple, and they ask, "By what authority are you doing these things?" The discourse sets the audience up to hear its frequent messianic claims echoing in their minds when the women at the end "say nothing to anyone."

In addition to its use of silence to draw attention to the question of who Jesus is, the rhetorical strategy of silence at the end of Mark's Gospel reverses plotted expectations in the narrative to create a daring turn to the reader whom the discourse has readied to speak what the narrative leaves unsaid. In Mark 9:9 Jesus specifies "after he has risen from the dead" as the time to tell the secret of his messianic identity. With the young man's proclamation in Mark 16:6 that Jesus is risen, the time for telling the secret arrives. In the next verse the young man explicitly commissions the women to tell Jesus' disciples and Peter that Jesus goes ahead of them to Galilee in accordance with the prophecy Jesus made in 14:28. Rhetorically, the women's silence in 16:8b, "And they said nothing to anyone because they were afraid," reverses the plotted expectation of 9:9 and 16:7.

A feminist hermeneutics that keeps women at the center of biblical interpretation recognizes that the young man in 16:7 sends the women not to the twelve but to "his disciples" (*tois mathētais autou*). A feminist perspective remembers that Mark 15:41 places many women among those who followed and served Jesus and came with him to Jerusalem, so the term *mathētais autou* includes both men and women disciples. Feminist hermeneutics questions why the text specifies Peter as the only individual to whom the women should tell the good news. The response that he is the leader of the disciples is a possible but patriarchal answer. Pursuing the question further reveals that the Markan plot suspends the named men disciples in silence earlier in the plot, just as it does the women at the end. As a character in the Gospel, Peter follows Jesus farther along his journey to the cross than any of the other disciples except the women. The narrative leaves Peter weeping in 14:72, having realized that he has three times denied Jesus. Jesus prophesied that this would happen; in fact, in Mark 14:27–30, Jesus makes three prophecies, each having to do with following him.

14:27 "You will all become deserters for it is written, 'I will strike the shepherd and the sheep will scatter.'"

14:28 "After I am raised up, I will go before you into Galilee."

14:30 "This very night before the cock crows twice, you will deny me three times."

Indeed, in Mark 14:50, when guards arrest Jesus, his disciples fulfill the first prophecy (A). When the disciples' actions fulfill Jesus' words, they drop out of the plot. In Mark 14:72 Peter remembers Jesus' third prophecy (C), "Before the cock crows twice, you will deny me three times"; he breaks down and weeps. The narrative leaves Peter in this scene but reminds hearers and readers to remember him when the young man in 16:7, whose good news repeats Jesus' third prophecy in 14:28 (B), tells the women Jesus has gone ahead to Galilee and to tell his disciples and Peter. Peter is a round character in the Gospel, whose journey in faith is most fully developed in the narrative.[3] He follows Jesus unhesitantly in Galilee, speaks for the group in confessing that Jesus is the messiah, fails to fathom that the messiah must suffer and die, insists that he will die rather than betray Jesus, but denies him without realizing it. The good news that Jesus is risen and once again gone ahead of his disciples

will redescribe these moments of failure in the plot. Peter can follow Jesus
again. The disciples can gather around their risen shepherd. But such ful-
fillment of plotted expectation describes a fairy-tale ending, not the way
and truth of those who follow the crucified messiah. The young man in
the tomb testifies to the truth of the third prophecy, but the silence of the
women leaves its claim for the audience to appropriate and proclaim. The
young man's proclamation that Jesus is risen fulfills Jesus' prophecy in all
three passion predictions that he would rise on the third day (8:30; 9:31;
10:34). The women's silence suspends the narrative with plotted expectations that Jesus will rise from the dead fulfilled and the time to tell the
secret at hand.

This study sees in the silence of Jesus' closest women and men disciples rhetorical purpose rather than reference to the historical failure of his
earliest disciples. In making fear and silence the unexpected response of
the faithful women in Mark 16:8b—but also the consistent and characteristic response of the specially chosen, named men disciples—the first
Gospel constructs a conclusion to persuade its readers to speak their own
faith and commitment and carry out the commission that the women
characters in the narrative do not fulfill.

By reversing plotted expectations and suspending the ending in faithful disciples' unexpected fear and silence, the Gospel lets its repeated
christological claims echo in the readers' minds and lets a new generation
know how timidly Jesus' earliest disciples began their ministry. The early
disciples well known in Christian tradition—Peter, James, and John and
Mary Magdalene, Mary the mother of James and Joses, and Salome—
never tell who Jesus is in the story. This is what pushes interpreters such
as Mary Ann Tolbert to see both Jesus' male and female disciples as failures and to project an ideal response onto the audience.[4] In contrast to
the silence of those specially instructed and commissioned to tell the
good news, four anonymous suppliants whom Jesus heals do tell all he
has done for them. Two of these—the leper in 1:24 and the deaf mute in
7:36—are characters Jesus enjoins to keep the secret of his identity. One
is the woman with the hemorrhage, who overcomes her fear to tell the
whole truth of the healing. The fourth is the Gerasene demoniac, whom
Jesus frees and sends to preach in the Decapolis area. The first Gospel
deliberately silences the eyewitness generation, both the men and women
disciples who spread the good news of Jesus' resurrection and messianic
identity. Instead it gives voice to four anonymous preachers and deliberately addresses the reader or hearer with silence their own witness can
speak.

CHAPTER 8

Calling a New Generation

꧁꧂

He is going ahead of you. (Mark 16:7)

MARK'S GOSPEL not only suspends Mary Magdalene, Mary the Mother of James and Joses, and Salome in fear and silence at its original ending in 16:8; it also suspends Peter, James, John, and other men disciples in fear and silence at other points in the narrative. These first-generation, eyewitness disciples all keep Jesus' messianic identity secret. In Mark's Gospel, no one important enough for tradition to remember his or her name preaches Jesus' resurrection from the dead or testifies that he is the Christ, the Son of God, the Gospel's announced purpose in its first verse. However, four anonymous suppliants, persons whom Jesus heals or frees in the narrative but whose names tradition does not remember, do preach and give witness about Jesus, and, of course, so does the written narrative itself. In this deliberately constructed contrast between silent and bold-speaking characters, this study finds an interpretative key to the first Gospel.

What best accounts for this contrast is not the actual, historical failure of Jesus' first disciples but the needs of those for whom the first Gospel was written—for a fearful and hesitant new generation of hearers in 70 C.E. who know that discipleship may mean persecution and can cost one's life, who no longer have the Jerusalem temple as a religious center, and who are experiencing the eyewitnesses being martyred or growing old and unable to carry on. The destruction of the temple, which the Jewish historian Josephus describes, ends Christianity's continuity with Israel's ancient religious practice. The Christian community becomes the temple not made with hands which the witnesses against Jesus at his trial claim he said he would build (Mark 14:58). The dying of the eyewitness generation of Jesus' disciples distances the Christian community from its origins. The rhetoric of Mark's Gospel speaks to a new generation who never knew Jesus, who can no longer count on his eyewitnesses to be with them, and who have not committed themselves to continuing Jesus' mission. The fear and silence of Jesus' first disciples in the Gospel make sense in this intergenerational context. The author of Mark's Gospel chooses to characterize Jesus' first disciples in their initial awestruck fear and confusion about who Jesus is rather than in their heroic maturity as long-dedicated leaders or martyrs who have given their lives to continuing Jesus' mission during the ensuing forty years. The choice the first Gospel urges upon its hearers is faith and active proclamation of the good news of Jesus. It urges them to take their place among the prophetic leaders throughout Israel's history, to walk the way of the Holy One that Second Isaiah first preached six hundred years earlier and John the Baptist prepared for Jesus, to follow in the footsteps of Jesus' first disciples as they followed Jesus himself. The faith of past generations is always at risk in the rising up of every new generation of believers—in 70 C.E., and today.

Werner Kelber recognizes that Mark's Gospel implies an intergenerational context as the first stable, written Gospel takes the place of fluid oral forms of tradition.[1] His interest, however, lies in the history behind the text. Kelber explains this media shift as a linguistic plot to both silence oral authorities—namely, Jesus' family, Christian preacher-prophets, and the first generation of Jesus' disciples—and reorient Christians toward the crucified and risen Jesus, who is at the center of the Gospel text.[2] For Kelber, the text embodies the historical Jesus as a corrective for disciples for whom superhero theology about Jesus has replaced his historical identity as the crucified messiah. Kelber proposes that the destruction of Jerusalem in 70 C.E. and the resulting upheaval for the Christian community in Jerusalem provide catalysts for the composition of the first Gospel, which recenters Jesus' story in Galilee after his death in Jerusalem.

> The cataclysmic loss of the center called into serious question the orally perceived presence of the Lord, awakening doubts about oral heroic christology and distrust of oral authorities. The new medium engineered the textual retrieval of Jesus' past authority, producing a literary representation that still displayed the deep wound of the oral absence of the Lord.[3]

Kelber identifies Jesus' first disciples and family members, whom the Gospel casts in negative roles, with those in the historical community whom the Markan written text wants to criticize. However, the media shift so absorbs Kelber that he credits the author and text rather than death and martyrdom with silencing early authorities. Kelber rightly perceives an intergenerational dynamic behind the shift from oral to written Gospel, but, without literary and rhetorical tools of analysis, misinterprets the failure and silence of Jesus' earliest, best-known, named disciples as characters in the narrative.

A literary perspective that recognizes that the written Gospel aims to communicate with a reader or hearer ahead of the text and a rhetorical perspective that recognizes that the text must address the needs of its readers in order to persuade them to believe and act can reconstruct from the rhetorical strategies crafted into the narrative the impact the text intends to have on readers and hearers. In suspending key story characters in the narrative—most male disciples in flight, Peter in tears at the high priest's courtyard, the faithful women in silence and fear—the rhetoric of the discourse creates signature scenes which emphasize the experience of characters most relevant to the audience. Rhetorical focus on the male disciples' flight, Peter's regret, and the women disciples' fear and silence suggest that the audience of the first Gospel is struggling with flight, regret, fear, and silence. If the implied author of the text is correctly reading what impedes the audience from acting, the first hearers of Mark's Gospel have fled danger or persecution, feel regret, live in fear, and hesitate to take up the proclamation of the Gospel, which is the expressed content of the written narrative (1:1). This picture fits with the future to which Jesus calls his followers in Mark 13:9–13, when he charges prophetically that before the world ends "the gospel must first be proclaimed to all nations" (13:10) but that persecution will result. What the audience in 70 C.E. needs to know about Jesus' earliest and best-known men and women disciples is not that after Jesus' resurrection they followed and served him, giving their lives to the preaching of the gospel, but that their discipleship began in flight, regret, fear, and silence. The first word of the Markan text (*archē*) points to the narrative's focus on one particular moment in discipleship—its beginning. For an audience in 70 C.E., the story's focus on the beginning of the named men's and women's discipleship can play against their extratextual knowledge of these faithful disciples in the forty years after Jesus' death and resurrection and before the writing of the Gospel. The narrative can silence the women at its conclusion because the audience knows they did indeed tell the good news but also knows they have died or grown too old to continue the work of proclamation, and thus the narrative calls its audience in 70 C.E. to continue the work they can no longer do. This is the work that Jesus lays out in Mark 13:10 in a chapter that sets Jesus up to speak prophetically both to his disciples in the story and to the hearers of the narrative. The leper, the mute, the Gerasene demoniac, and the woman healed of hemorrhage are anonymous disciples who model the work of proclaiming Jesus for the listeners of the written story. Perhaps the last two verses of Mark's Gospel spoke so directly to the needs of the original audience and depended so entirely on that audience's own knowledge of the first disciples' lived-out commitments that its original ending proved timebound. However, the new written Gospel genre proved too valuable not to fix. Other writers edit and add to create whole new Gospels that focus less on the *archē* of faith and discipleship than on christological reflection and Christian mission.

What in the literary text and rhetoric argues for this interpretation? First, Mark's Gospel gives the named men and women positive eyewitness roles in the narrative, not only negative characteristics. Second, the narrative puts Peter, James, and John in an intergenerational context at several points and alludes to their post-Easter discipleship. Third, the narrative has four anonymous disciples testify to Jesus' healing power in their lives, a role that fulfills the challenge the narrative extends to its audience.

NAMED MEN AND WOMEN EYEWITNESS CHARACTERS

Besides making Mary Magdalene and the other women eyewitnesses of Jesus' death, burial, and resurrection, the narrative also puts Peter, James, and John alone with Jesus at three scenes mirroring these same events— Jesus' raising of Jairus's daughter, his transfiguration in glory, and his prayer in the garden of Gethsemane just before his arrest. Christological proclamations fall silent in the first Gospel with the centurion's remark, "Surely this was the Son of God." From this point on in the narrative, the women disciples have the positive role of witnessing the events that Jesus three times prophesies (8:32; 9:34; and 10:32) and that the Christian creed recites, "He was crucified, died, and was buried, and on the third day he arose again. . . ." Paul names these same events in 1 Corinthians 15:3–5, the earliest New Testament creedal statement:

> I delivered to you as of first importance what I also received, that Christ died for our sins in accordance with the scriptures, that he was buried, that he was raised on the third day in accordance with scriptures and that he

appeared to Cephas, then to the twelve, then to more than five hundred brethren at one time.

Both Mary Magdalene and Peter have essential roles in all four written Gospels. All four Gospels place Mary Magdalene at the crucifixion, burial, and discovery of the empty tomb, making her a nonnegotiable essential character in the Gospel. This consistency argues that her narrative role represents her historical activity. This argument makes Mary Magdalene as important in the Gospel traditions as the twelve, whom likewise all four Gospels include in their narratives, and as essential as Peter, who in each Gospel denies Jesus and regrets it. Peter's denial and Mary's witness are essential to the Gospel story. That the rhetoric of the Markan narrative suspends both story characters in negative moments—Peter weeping in regret and Mary Magdalene silent and afraid—does not negate the women's importance as eyewitnesses of Jesus' death, burial, and resurrection and the men's importance as eyewitnesses of Jesus' ministry and journey to the cross.

Jesus calls Peter, Andrew, James, and John to follow him in Mark 1:16–20; these four witness Jesus' preaching, healing, and casting out demons from the beginning. The men disciples ask him questions and receive instruction from him in crowds and in private. The narrative names Peter, James, and John as the only witnesses of two scenes—the raising of Jairus's daughter, in which Jesus demonstrates power like the power God shows in raising Jesus from the dead, and the transfiguration, in which they glimpse Jesus in risen glory. In addition, the three accompany Jesus to pray in the garden, where they sleep through his coming to terms with the cup of suffering and death. The narrative calls Peter, James, and John out of the group to witness the events of Jesus' ministry that are closest to the resurrection, anticipating the risen presence of Jesus with them, which the suspended ending of Mark never narrates. Like the named women, Peter, James, and John have eyewitness importance in their narrative roles that contrasts with their fear and silence in Mark's rhetoric.[4]

PETER, JAMES, AND JOHN IN INTERGENERATIONAL CONTEXT

The eyewitness characters Peter, James, and John appear in scenes in the first Gospel that clearly have an intergenerational context. Mark's Gospel evokes five historical time periods in its narrative (see fig. 5). Through allusions to and quotations of Israel's scriptures and the story of John the Baptist's beheading, the narrative evokes Israel's prophetic history from Moses to John the Baptist. This is the *background time* against which the Markan narrative tells the story of Jesus' brief ministry, death, and resurrection. Jesus' ministry takes place around 30 C.E. in history; this is the *story time*. The purpose that shapes the composition of the first written Gospel reflects a later time period, probably after the Romans' destruction of the temple in 70 C.E. Jesus' description of the temple with not one stone upon another (Mark 13:3) is one reason for dating the writing of the Gospel after 70 C.E. This means that the *writing time*, about 70 C.E., was four decades later than the story time. Anyone who was twenty at the time of Jesus' death and resurrection was sixty at the time of the writing of the Gospel. Undoubtedly many eyewitnesses to the events the Gospel story narrates were dead. Tradition holds that Peter died a martyr in 64 C.E. during persecutions Nero initiated in Rome and no later than 67 C.E.[5] The writing orients Jesus' story toward an audience in 70 C.E. who can continue the work of Jesus' first disciples. Between the story time and the writing time is the *mission time* of Jesus' first disciples, their giving of their lives to the gospel. The named men disciples appear in the Gospel as pre-Easter followers of Jesus who misunderstand his teachings and fail to walk with him to the cross, rather than in their post-Easter willingness to give their lives to the gospel. However, Acts knows Peter as a missionary and leader of the early Christian community and James as a martyred leader of the church in Jerusalem. The *Gospel of Thomas* and the *Gospel of Mary* include Mary Magdalene among Jesus' inner circle of disciples and portray her as a rival of Peter, which suggests that she too gave her life to the spreading of the gospel. In addition to these four historical periods in the Gospel, children bring up a fifth—*future time*. The Markan narrative, then, evokes five time frames and portrays characters who belong to each period (see fig. 5).

The narrative so collapses these time periods that only occasionally, as in the case of the three scenes with Peter, James, and John, do the historical layers become perceptible. These scenes in Mark 5:22–43, 9:1–13, and 14:32–42 even hint at these disciples' post-Easter commitments.

THE RAISING OF JAIRUS'S DAUGHTER

Peter, James, and John stand in an intergenerational context when they witness the raising of Jairus's daughter. The healing of a woman who has hemorrhaged for twelve years takes place between two segments of the story about Jesus' raising a synagogue leader's twelve-year-old daughter from apparent death (5:22–43). Jesus calls Peter, James, and John from among his disciples to accompany him to Jairus's home, when the news arrives in the second half of the story that his daughter is not just sick but dead (5:37). This Markan sandwich or intercalation forms the center of the chiasm schematized in figure 12, chapter 10. A twenty-verse exorcism of the Gerasene demoniac immediately precedes the healing of the woman and the girl, a liberation that makes witnesses so afraid that they ask Jesus to leave their region. In the story following the raising of Jairus's daughter, the people of Jesus' hometown synagogue reject his preaching. These two stories contrast Gentile faith and hometown Jewish rejection, making it significant that the man who asks Jesus to save his daughter is a synagogue leader. The doublet stories that frame this chiasm are the two sea-crossing stories—Jesus' quieting of the storm that threatens his disciples (4:35–41) and his appearance walking on the water (6:34–44) (A, A'). Between these stories is a second intercalation and a second intergenerational context, the story of the beheading of John the Baptist, which the author places between Jesus' sending out his own disciples to preach, heal, and expel demons and their coming back.

Figure 5: Markan Time Periods

Historical Time	Narrative Time	Characters
1200 B.C.E.–30 C.E.	Prophetic past	Moses, Elijah, Isaiah, John the Baptist
30 C.E.	Story time	Jesus, first men and women disciples.
30–70 C.E.	Mission time	Eyewitness men and women disciples
70 C.E.	Writing time	Nameless suppliants who preach, witness
After 70 C.E.	Future time	Children

The first intercalation—a miracle story within a miracle story—has three intergenerational pairs: Jairus and his dying daughter, Jesus and the healed woman whom he addresses as daughter, and the woman who has hemorrhaged for twelve years and the girl dying at twelve, the age of menses.

The second story within a story also has intergenerational pairs. Jesus, the teacher, sends out disciples to do what he has been doing, namely, preach, heal, and cast out demons. This is a teacher/disciple intergenerational relationship. The beheaded John the Baptist prefigures the rejection both Jesus and his disciples will face; he is precursor to those who follow, another intergenerational relationship. A family causes John the Baptist's death. He criticizes Herod for marrying his sister-in-law Herodias, who has her daughter call for John's head. The two healed daughters in the first intercalation contrast with the murderous mother/daughter pair in the second.

The woman at the center of the first story within a story speaks in the midst of her community the whole truth of her healing and becomes in the narrative one of the anonymous preachers who provide hearers in 70 C.E. with a model response. From the center of the second story within a story, John the Baptist testifies to the price of his preaching, which antedates Jesus' own death. Between the sea-crossing doublets Mark creates a procession of prophets and disciples who come from various time periods: John the Baptist, Jesus, Jesus' disciples, the demoniac, the anonymous woman, and the girl raised up to life.

Figure 6: Time Periods in Mark 4:35–6:52

Historical Time	Narrative Time	Characters
Prior to 30 C.E.	Prophetic past	John the Baptist
30 C.E.	Story time	Jesus preaches, heals, and casts out demons, sends disciples to do the same. Peter, James, and John witness Jesus raise Jairus's daughter.
30–70 C.E.	Mission time	The disciples' mission in the Gospel anticipates their post-Easter mission.
70 C.E.	Writing time	Woman healed of hemorrhage testifies in community. Demoniac preaches to Gerasenes.
After 70 C.E.	Future	Jairus's daughter lives toward the future.

The first story within a story reaches forward in time; the second reaches backward in history. The presence of Peter, James, and John at the raising of Jairus's daughter places them, like the women in Mark 16:8, as silent witnesses of a resurrection. The woman who testifies in the eye of the story models the response the discourse expects of its hearers. The story-time disciples who became mission-time preachers and witnesses stand silent in the narrative that was written to call hearers in 70 C.E. to follow both Jesus and his first disciples.

THE TRANSFIGURATION

The second intergenerational scene in which Peter, James, and John appear is the story of the transfiguration (9:1–13). The narrative weaves this scene carefully into the section framed by doublet healings of blind men (8:22–26; 10:45–52). Jesus' three passion predictions orient this section both thematically and geographically toward his death and resurrection in Jerusalem, setting up a journey toward the cross at the midpoint of the narrative.

In scenes leading up to the transfiguration, Jesus first heals a blind man in two stages, a miracle that suggests Jesus' disciples have to grow into deeper insight about who Jesus really is. When Jesus puts saliva on the man's eyes he begins to see in a blurry fashion—the people around him appear as trees. Jesus touches his eyes a second time and he sees clearly (8:22–26). This miracle comes immediately before Jesus questions his disciples about who people say he is and asks, "Who do you say that I am?" Peter responds, "You are the messiah." The narrative places Peter's profession that Jesus is the messiah back to back with a scene in which Jesus first predicts his passion and Peter objects, revealing that his vision of Jesus is still blurry. After the narrative catches Peter with much more to learn about who Jesus is, it tucks in before the transfiguration story several sayings that invite those who want to follow Jesus to take up their cross and that promise that those who lose their lives will find them. These sayings speak to later disciples in mission time and writing time. Jesus' disciples in story time are following him to the cross although they cannot yet envision a messiah who suffers. The Markan narrative composition weaves Peter, James, and John into an intergenerational context, in which the prophetic past, story time, mission, and writing time become distinguishable.

Figure 7: Time Periods in Mark (8:22–26; 10:45–52)

Prophetic Past	*Story Time*	*Mission Time*	*Writing Time*
	8:22–26 Jesus heals blind man.		
	8:27–30 Peter "You are the messiah."		
	8:31–33 Peter objects to first passion prediction		
		8:34–9:1 Whoever desires to come after me must take up their cross and follow me. Those who lose their lives for my sake or the sake of the gospel will find them.	
9:4 Jesus speaks with Moses, Elijah	**9:2–8** Peter, James, John see Jesus in risen glory	**9:9** Tell what you have seen after I have risen.	
9:9–13 Elijah has come and people did what they wanted with him.			

The sayings in 8:34–9:1 address post-Easter disciples during the forty years of mission time and at the writing time who did not make the journey to the cross with Jesus. The transfiguration scene itself evokes both the prophetic past in the persons of Moses and Elijah, who appear with Jesus in glory, and the post-Easter mission time during which Jesus commissions the three disciples to tell about the glory they have seen. Jesus' remarks imply that John the Baptist is Elijah come again, rejected and mistreated as Elijah was (1 Kings 19). Peter, James, and John question what rising from the dead can mean but keep the vision secret (9:10). This scene silences the three named men disciples, who for the second time witness a kind of resurrection in this vision, just as it silences the women in 16:8b. At its midpoint, Mark's Gospel lines up an intergenerational procession of disciples that reaches backward and forward in history—Moses, Elijah,

John the Baptist, Jesus, Peter, James, John, and all those who take up their crosses and lose their lives for the sake of the gospel.

After the third passion prediction, which Jesus makes on the road to Jerusalem (10:32–34), but before the second healing of a blind man ends this narrative section (10:45–52), Jesus has a private conversation with James and John (10:35–45). This conversation echoes Peter's objection to Jesus' first passion prediction. James and John ask to sit at Jesus' left and right hand in his glory, which they witnessed in the transfiguration scene. Jesus tells them they don't know what they are asking and challenges them with the question "Are you able to drink the cup I drink, or be baptized with the baptism that I am baptized with?" (10:38). They say, "We can." Ekkehard Stegemann hears in the phrase "the cup I drink" a "formula of martyrdom,"[6] which receives its full meaning in the third scene that places Peter, James, and John with Jesus—the agony in the garden.

THE AGONY IN THE GARDEN

In Mark 14:32–42 Peter, James, and John accompany Jesus to the garden, where he prays, "Abba, Father, for you all things are possible, remove this cup from me" (14:36). Jesus goes to the garden to pray just after the meal, at which he takes a cup of wine, gives thanks, and passes the cup to his disciples who are at the supper with him. They drink from this cup, of which he says, "This is my blood of the covenant which is poured out for many" (14:24). The cup is Jesus' lifeblood and, for those who drink the cup he drinks, the pledge of martyrs' blood. In the garden Jesus prays to have the cup of his blood, his death, removed, but he accepts God's will and the scene ends with his arrest. Significantly, Peter, James, and John sleep through this scene. Jesus urges them to pray lest they be tempted. He urges them to watch. Stegemann argues that this scene evokes hearers' extratextual knowledge about Peter, James, and John. He suggests that the reason the initial four disciples have become three with Andrew not among them is that the audience knows of the martyrdoms of Peter and James so the narrative emphasizes them. "The choice of Peter, James, and John finds its explanation in that they are the disciples of Jesus whom the reader knows as martyrs and participants in his destiny in a narrower sense."[7]

Through the image of the cup, the narrative places Peter, James, and John in the line of prophets that begins with Moses and Elijah, which

John the Baptist and Jesus continue, and which the written story calls its hearers to join. Prophets suffer rejection and often death. Peter, James, and John drink the cup of dedication unto martyrdom in the decades between Jesus' ministry and the writing of the Gospel. The rhetoric of the Gospel presumes that its hearers know that Jesus' eyewitness disciples fearlessly preached his good news to the nations, but it also knows that the eyewitnesses no longer proclaim the gospel in 70 C.E. Their keeping of the secret in Mark's story presumes their preaching mission in history but recognizes that time and martyrdom have silenced their voices. The written Gospel calls new disciples to take their place.

The first Gospel begins with John the Baptist preparing Jesus' way (1:2–8) and echoing Second Isaiah's earlier prophetic call to prepare the way for God's manifestation. The Gospel ends with sixteen verses in which women who followed and served Jesus in Galilee and who came with him to Jerusalem follow him to the cross, to his burial, and to his proclaimed resurrection. Both prologue and epilogue are integral to the main narrative. In the prologue, the author of Mark's Gospel identifies John the Baptist's preaching, which prepares Jesus' way, with the voice of Second Isaiah calling the people of Israel in exile to prepare a way for God to lead them home as God earlier led their ancestor on a dry path through the sea. In the epilogue the young man in white at the empty tomb on Easter morning announces that the risen Jesus continues on the way ahead of his disciples as he promised. The narrative shows readers and hearers that the Jesus who walks ahead of his disciples to Jerusalem still goes ahead of them and will be with them in Galilee, to which Christians fled from Jerusalem during the rebellion against Rome (66–70 C.E.).[8] The author of Mark expects hearers in 70 C.E. to recognize that Jesus' first disciples experienced flight, fear, regret, and confused silence like their own as it urges them to take up Jesus' cross and proclaim the gospel of his resurrection, to step beyond their fear and confusion to faith and proclamation. In Mark's Gospel the women and men of the first generation of Jesus' followers call the women and men of the next generation to continue the work of spreading the gospel.

FOUR ANONYMOUS PREACHERS

Four disciples in the Markan narrative testify to Jesus' healing power in their lives. All are anonymous, which suggests that the discourse sees them not only as suppliants in story time but as role models for its audience at the time the Gospel was written. The leper (1:44), the Gerasene set free of a legion of demons (5:20), the woman healed of hemorrhage (5:33), and the deaf mute set free to speak (8:36) tell the messianic secret that the men and women eyewitnesses can no longer proclaim. The leper and deaf mute are two among those Jesus enjoins not to tell who he is, but who do so anyway. Jesus refuses to let the Gerasene follow him but sends him to his own people to preach (5:19). The story refers to Jesus with the post-Easter designation Lord (*Kyrios*). The man "began to preach (*kēryssein*) in the Decapolis how much Jesus had done for him."

All four of these anonymous suppliants who testify are social outsiders. Jewish religious law made lepers social outcasts to prevent spread of the contagious disease and made women ritually unclean during menstruation. The leper lived outside society. The woman with the hemorrhage could not participate in religious cultic practice. The Gerasene lived among the dead, unable to join in society. The deaf mute had no language with which to take part in society. Their healings free them to become insiders. Each has Jesus' healing power to tell others about. The leper and the woman with the hemorrhage are Galilean Jews; the Gerasene and deaf mute live in the Gentile Decapolis area and are probably Gentiles.

In her feminist interpretation, Marla Selvidge finds the woman healed of a hemorrhage a significant member, role determiner, and voice of God to the community. Mark's sandwiching of her story in the middle of the girl's and the similarities between the two miracle stories convince Selvidge the stories belong together.[9] Both women are daughters. Jesus addresses the woman as daughter (5:34); the synagogue leader asks healing for his daughter (5:23). Menstruation and the number twelve figure in both stories. The woman has been afflicted for twelve years with a menstrual problem, which Mark terms a scourge (*mastigos*). Acts 22:24 and Hebrews 11:36 use this word to mean whippings or scourgings.[10] Her flow of blood makes her unclean and places her outside Jewish cult; her healing closes the breach between woman and cult.[11] Jairus's daughter is twelve (5:42), the age of puberty. The onset of menstruation is about to jeopardize her participation in the cult, in which her father is a leader.

The woman claims Jesus' healing power for herself by touching his garment, not Jesus himself, suggesting historical distance from the flesh-and-blood Jesus. When Jesus wants to know who touched him, she trembles fearfully but comes before him in the midst of the crowd and disciples, falls down, and tells the whole truth of her healing—she speaks a word of faith in the community. In Mark the word *haima* is used only of the woman's flow of blood and Jesus' blood of the new covenant. The Gospel parallels her suffering and Jesus' scourging before his death. The woman qualifies as model and leader; her affliction connects her with Jesus' suffering and all suffering.[12] This story within a story makes the woman's testimony to healing from long physical suffering, social isolation, and religious uncleanness the interpretative key to the resurrection of a young woman. The older woman's voice testifies to women's place in the next generation of Jesus' disciples, a call the young woman has been set free to follow in the future.

CONCLUSION

The rhetoric of Mark's suspended ending plays to an audience experiencing a transition between the eyewitness generation of Jesus' followers, who are growing old or have already been martyred, and themselves—a potential new generation of Christians. The deaths of the women and men who followed and served Jesus in his lifetime and proclaimed his gospel to the world coincide with the Roman destruction of the temple, which uproots the community of Jesus' followers in Jerusalem. Some of Jesus' first followers have drunk the cup their leader drank, making clear to younger Christians that persecution may be their inheritance as it was Jesus' destiny and that of some of his earliest disciples. Markan rhetoric pictures Jesus' earliest women and men disciples in the numinous fear and liminal silence where their faith and commitment began as persuasive encouragement for its hearers to take up their mission. The failure of both the women and men disciples in the Markan story does not refer to their failure in history; it is instead Markan rhetoric that deheroicizes Mary Magdalene, Mary the mother of Joses and James, Salome, Peter, James, and John in order to persuade its hearers to take the first step out of mute fear in a journey that could end in martyrdom.

The women of Galilee in Mark 15:40–41, 47 and 16:1–8 are disciples of Jesus who faithfully follow and serve him from the beginning of the first day of his ministry, when Peter's mother-in-law serves him, to the day of his death on the cross, his burial, and beyond. They follow Jesus farther than all other characters in the narrative. They witness the crucifixion. They see where Jesus is buried. They take on the work of rolling back the gravestone and giving Jesus' body a proper anointing, which the narrative has an unnamed woman prophetically accomplish (14:6), anointing Jesus as messiah rather than for death.

Mark's Gospel treats Jesus' early named women and men disciples with remarkable consistency as story characters. The narrative in 4:41, 6:52, 9:6, 9:32, and 10:32 deliberately suspends Jesus' first men disciples in numinous fear much the way the final six words suspend the women disciples in 16:8b. The discourse makes these same women and men disciples the most reliable keepers of the secret that Jesus is the messiah, the Son of God. At the same time, the written Gospel repeatedly echoes messianic claims about Jesus across the narrative and has four anonymous suppliants spread the good news of their healing.

The woman freed of hemorrhage moves beyond numinous fear to faith and proclamation of the whole truth of her healing in the midst of the community. The leper from Galilee and the deaf mute from the Decapolis area cannot keep quiet. Jesus himself sends the fourth suppliant, the Gerasene demoniac, on a mission to tell his own people what the Lord has done for him.

The women's concluding fear and silence have rhetorical purpose. In this reversal of plotted expectations, the most faithful disciples in the narrative stand in fear and silence in order to coax the hearers of the story to a performative response that the historical disciples whom these story characters represent can no longer continue. The narrative pictures these exemplary disciples in their vulnerable, and therefore more imitable, initial response to Jesus' absence and their call to mission. Feminist hermeneutics, which decenters interpretation from Jesus and his men followers, finds women disciples of equal importance in the narrative. With the warrants of feminist hermeneutics, which keep the women disciples at the center of interpretation, and the warrants of literary-critical tools, which function in decoding the narrative and its rhetoric, this study hears in the first written Gospel a christological catechesis and a call to proclamation. The rhetorical strategy of freezing the women disciples in silence and fear calls for a performative response—for hearers of this word to do what the women witnesses can no longer do. The daughter who speaks the whole truth of Jesus' healing her of hemorrhage models the future participation of the audience in the mission of the Jesus movement. Jairus's daughter raised to new life suggests a future for women in the community which no longer regularly excludes them from worship for carrying within them the blood of human life.

As a written work, the potential meanings and uses of the first Gospel overflow its original purposes. Its alternative endings and the other three Gospels rewrite this first Gospel and eliminate its original ending for later generations who did not bring the requisite extratextual knowledge of the eyewitness generation to the hearing of their fear and silence in the story. The rewritings subordinate the women eyewitnesses to the men and tame its rhetorical dynamics, creating written works that are more objective, orderly, timeless, and less dependent on hearers to perform their charge. The rhetoric of the original Markan ending offers a much-needed model of catechesis that calls its hearers to participate in interpreting the story and performing its commission.

CHAPTER 9

Narrative and Reader

❦

IRONICALLY, THE SUNDAY LECTIONARY, which provides the scripture readings for the Roman Catholic community of faith in which this writer worships, never reads Mark 16:8. The lectionary reads Mark 16:1–7 at the Easter Vigil in cycle B and suggests it as an alternative reading to John 20:1–10 on Easter Sunday, cycle B. The church gives the verse to which this study has given so much attention no occasion for public Sunday proclamation. Contemporary Bibles supply the Gospel of Mark with an alternative ending. Few hear the ancient rhetoric of Mark's last verse, which suspends the history-like illusion inherent in narrative and addresses the whole Gospel to the hearer to finish the work of interpreting its meaning and completing its unfulfilled commission. Feminist interpreter Joanna Dewey concludes that the women are seen but not heard.

Mark 16:8 makes explicit what is true of all written narrative. It addresses an audience in an author's stead. As a written and crafted literary genre, a narrative leaves the author for a life of its own in dialogue with its receivers. The first Gospel and the individual who wrote it stand nearly two millennia distant from the communities of Christians who receive it today. A long stream of interpretation flows from this Gospel and a long line of the Christian communities it has constituted over the centuries. We receive the Gospel in a far more complex context than the first audience, whose original hearing is impossible to wholly recover. With all its need for interpretation, the Gospel travels through time as a lasting and stabilizing story from which Christians can construct identity.

Without feminist-resistant and generative reading, the other Synoptic Gospels and the alternative ending of Mark trivialize the witness of the women disciples and obscure their presence as equals among Jesus' first disciples. If Jesus' company is exclusively male, sermons and religious education can hold up only male mirrors of discipleship. Feminists have at stake in Bible interpretation both women's participation in the original Jesus movement and women's agency today as capable interpreters and preachers of the word. Mark's Gospel provides present communities of reception with both a summons to dialogue in 16:8 (the subject of this chapter) and a model of emancipatory dialogue in 7:24–30 (the subject of the next chapter).

NARRATIVE INVITES DIALOGUE

For most people the word dialogue implies face-to-face conversation. When an author speaks through a narrative to readers and hearers at a distance, the author invites dialogue but with the narrative rather than face to face with himself or herself. Applying Julia Kristeva's linguistic analysis[1] to Mark 16:6–8 will help make the relationships among author, narrative, and reader clear. This scene begins inside the empty tomb; a young man addresses three women from Galilee who come to anoint Jesus' body:

> (6) He said to them, "Do not be amazed; you seek Jesus of Nazareth, who was crucified. He has risen, he is not here; see the place where they laid him. (7) But go, tell his disciples and Peter that he is going before you to Galilee; there you will see him, as he told you." (8) And they went out and fled from the tomb; for trembling and astonishment had come upon them; and they said nothing to anyone, for they were afraid. (Mark 16:6–8)

The women don't respond to the conversation the young man initiates in this scene. Kristeva's analysis directs us to recognize two invisible dialogues taking place behind this scene. First, an author is addressing an audience. In Kristeva's terminology, a written narrative sets up a dialogue between a subject (author) and an addressee (audience).

Figure 8

Author	-----	Audience
Subject		Addressee

Second, a narrator is addressing a reader. In a written narrative, the author becomes anonymous in the text; in the case of Mark, the author becomes the omniscient narrator from whose point of view the story unfolds. In other words, a narrative externalizes an author's address of an audience in a self-standing genre, a code, which the audience can decode at a distance from the author. The author of Mark becomes the omniscient narrator who is implicit in the composition of the plot, in characterization, in the rhetoric of the discourse. The audience does more than passively receive the story; audience members have an active role as signifiers or readers. The author becomes anonymous in a narrative genre, addressing the receiver of the narrative as a reader, one who can decode and interpret the genre. A second level of dialogue takes place within the first.[2]

Figure 9

Author ··· Audience

     Omniscient ················· Narrative ···················· Readers
        Narrator

For two verses in Mark (16:6–7) the omniscient narrator tells the story through the young man, the immediate narrator in the scene. He tells the three women characters the essentials that the entire Gospel proclaims: Jesus of Nazareth, who was crucified, is risen. A name for this essential message is the *kerygma*. The young man is a character in the story initiating a dialogue with other characters in the narrative, but his proclaiming of the kerygma to the women is also part of the dialogue the author intends with an audience, which takes place through the dialogue between omniscient narrator and reader.

Figure 10

Author ·· Audience

     Omniscient ·················· Narrative ···················· Readers
        Narrator

          Narrator ··············· Kerygma ···············Women
          Young Man

By not responding within the story, the women characters end its forward motion and suspend the history-like illusion that the story is taking place;

their silence allows the young man's words to address the reader instead. In fact, in the women's silence the narrative as a whole addresses the reader, who is the one the author wants to address and who can interpret the meaning of the narrative. The narrative expects dialogue of the reader. The narrative addresses the reader.

The distance between Jesus' first eyewitness followers and those in 70 C.E. continues to exist between each subsequent generation. As a written work, Mark's Gospel can continue to put the author in dialogue with indeterminate hearers ahead of the text, to whom this story can extend God's promises. In the intergenerational space its suspended ending creates, the first Gospel acknowledges that its story medium addresses its hearers and invites their response. This new Christian genre is a carnival of smaller story units, characters, sayings, and symbols that testify to the promise of Jesus Christ. This narrative world does the business of art to hold up mirrors to the reflecting self. The Gospel tells the story of Jesus and his early women and men disciples in order for readers to see and find themselves in the mirror of its literary world.

At the margin of the narrative, the women disciples become insiders with Jesus and the men, forming one generation, which the story puts in conversation with its hearers, who are outside its reality. The hearers of the new generation exist as insiders in a world beyond and outside the first generation's reality. The narrative is about generating meaning across separation.

Ultimately, individuals and communities take part from their specific social locations in the greater dialogue between Word and world, in which the Word incarnate in words must become emancipatory, transformative proclamation to and for the World.[3]

Figure 11

Word -- World

Author -- Audience

Omniscient ------------ Narrative ------------ Reader
Narrator

Narrator ---------- Kerygma ----------Women

HUMANS DEVELOP IN DIALOGUE

Both psychoanalyst D. W. Winnicott and linguist Julia Kristeva theorize that language arises in potential space, suggestive of the generative space the original ending of Mark creates for the reader. In adults, this liminal space becomes imagination, the threshold between our inside and outside worlds, where we can play with what is real and engage art and story. For both Winnicott and Kristeva, human beings construct reality in an intergenerational dialogue between self and caregiver, usually the mother. The dialogue takes place in what Winnicott terms a potential space between inside and outside, the place of imagination in older children and adults. Potential space is an intermediate area of experiencing between a child's inside mental representations and outside physical reality. Both inner reality and external life contribute to what happens in potential space.[4] Winnicott names such objects as teddy bears or satin edges of blankets "transitional objects," which children between four and twelve months use to defend against the absence of their mothers or constant caregivers. Winnicott observes in children who get "good-enough mothering" the emergence of these transitional objects, which allow the child to play with the mother or caregiver as object, as reality that is *not me*. The child uses an illusion or an imaginary object to test the external world. "The object represents the infant's transition from a state of being merged with the mother to a state of being in relation to the mother as an other outside and separate."[5] The baby creates an illusion that can substitute for the mother who is not there, but the baby cannot create the illusion if the mother does not reliably continue the illusion of merged identification with the infant, providing a trustworthy experience of the not-me, outside world.[6] All of this takes place in the potential space between a child's inner and outer world—"an infinite area of separation, which the baby, child, adolescent, adult may creatively fill with playing, which in time becomes the enjoyment of the cultural heritage."[7] The space between *me* and all that is *not me* is holy space. Without this separation, the self is its own god in a world coextensive with its ego; there is no outer/other reality. With separation, the experience of trustworthy adults helps the child develop potential space for recognizing and relating to all that is, liminal space in which one is also open to the ultimate Other.

From the point of view of psychology and faith development, the empty tomb and the women's silence create transitional space, the space between the inside reality of our experience and the outside social world of all others, including God, the ultimate, ineffable Other, the Nothing out of which all comes to be. Our images of God live in this potential space where imagination can dream them and destroy them when they no longer mediate God to us. In the final scene of the first Gospel the doorway between life and death stands ajar. The women characters carry their eyewitness experience inside the tomb and inside the narrative to hearers outside the tomb and the story, who must play in the potential space in which they can make meaning—in this case, believe.

The women who come to Jesus' tomb had experienced an unspeakable numbing event two days before. In the Easter scene in Mark 16:1–8 the mystery each woman is inside herself encounters dumbfounding Mystery outside. The psychic space the women inhabit is a gap. "At just this place of fearful crossing over from God as we imagine God to be and God revealing who God is, many of us lose faith," depth psychologist Ann Belford Ulanov explains.[8] In her working with people and their spiritual experience, Belford thinks:

> In religious life, we simply must reach this death place if we are to know that God lives. Just as the psyche presses us to enter those gaps in our self to become whole, so God presses us to enter this death place to receive new life.[9]

In exploring the origins of language in children, Julia Kristeva also analyzes how a child relates the inside to the outside world. Kristeva sees laughter as the first indicator that an infant recognizes an outer world. At two-and-a-half months, such sensations as those that accompany feeding, the light on the mother's face, or the sound of music become a *there*, a place outside the child which causes laughter from within. This delight signals the caregiver to repeat what makes the child laugh, which reinforces a growing sense of a stable, outside world.[10] At about three months the child projects the sensations to which it responds with laughter upon the face of the mother. A smile at the mother and first vocalizations develop contemporaneously. Once the caregiver's face becomes a point of psychic organization, the child slowly begins naming.[11] Naming, which Kristeva sees originating to express place, "is a *replacement* for what the speaker perceives as an archaic mother."[12] Recognizing a person outside the self and developing sounds from within the self to name the other happen together. Language develops to bridge separateness. A child develops the ability to play and name in order to locate the self socially, that is, in relation to all others. However, as children grow up, they learn language, discourses, religious and cultural symbols already signified in the outside environment. Their personal signifying ability can create new meaning, where received meanings become objectified or embody systemic distortions. Both Winnicott and Kristeva describe the human person as capable of play, naming, speaking, and using language to construct social reality. As Ana-Maria Rizzuto recognizes in her research in how children's images of God develop, each child has unique, historical experience out of which his or her images of God develop.[13] Every individual brings these private images of God and his or her own religious experience into any interpretive dialogue with a religious classic such as the Gospel.

As readers, human beings bring to a narrative the ability to decode the genre and to interpret its meaning for their lives. A narrative becomes a transitional object in the potential space of the human imagination, where a reader can test the fit between the world of the story and his or her own inner world.

CATECHESIS REQUIRES DIALOGUE

Catechetics is an activity that requires intergenerational dialogue. The noun *catechesis* means echoing, the echoing of Christian tradition, re-speaking it. Mark's first Gospel has this very purpose. In the Roman Catholic community, catechesis has as its aim to foster "active, conscious, living" faith.[14] Without a rhetoric that calls people in the present into dialogue with past traditions, catechesis becomes the handing on of information about the gospel, about Jesus, about his early disciples. Without recognizing that the gospel narrative addresses its audience as capable readers and interpreters, the Gospel becomes an artifact.

In the Roman Catholic Church, the Rite of Christian Initiation of Adults (RCIA) has reinstated an ancient practice in instructing new Christians. It makes the Gospels of the Sunday lectionary its primary source of catechesis. With Elisabeth Schüssler Fiorenza, ministers in parish RCIA groups seek to make the Gospels "bread not stone" for their hearers.[15] The phrase "breaking open the Word" expresses this purpose and makes a parallel between Christians gathering to break bread and to break open the word, both as nourishing sources of Christian identity. James B. Dunning describes adult initiation into the Christian community as a seven-stage process that prepares hearers to place the gospel in dialogue with their lives. Three steps precede exploring tradition, the step that includes dialogue with the gospel.

1. Storytelling, the sharing of life experience, and listening to that of others

2. Questioning that explores where I have come from, where I am going, and what my responsibilities are along the way

3. Finding companions who assure me I am not alone on my journey—forming communities of faith

4. Exploring tradition, which grounds us firmly in the roots of our history, scriptures, and gospel values

5. Conversion, an ongoing process of change and realization that my story is God's story

6. Celebration of God's presence and gifts in our lives, through prayer, Sunday liturgy, and the sacraments

7. Ministries, ways to use personal gifts to serve the people of God[16]

In the RCIA process, people raise their own questions, doubts, desires, and struggles together before they enter dialogue with the Gospels. The process uses this conversation to offset hearing the Gospel as fact and information rather than address and summons to conversion. It is a rhetorical model for today that does the work of Mark 16:8; it raises contemporary life concerns to which it expects the Gospel to speak.

As a conventional form of catechetical discourse, the catechism stands in opposition to the story as a means for communicating across generations. A catechism usually mimics dialogue on its surface in a question-and-answer format, but it answers the questions it asks within its discourse, defining and determining Christian faith in doctrinal propositions. *The Catechism of the Catholic Church* does not raise questions; its mission is "guarding the deposit of faith"[17] and "presenting an organic synthesis of the essential and fundamental contents of Catholic doctrine."[18] Its doctrinal contents number 2,865 paragraphs. A catechism may address readers but expects minimal participation in interpreting. It is more a vehicle for disseminating doctrinal norms.

Conversely, the first Gospel addresses the earliest community's christological claims about Jesus to the next generation as a narrative testimony its hearers must participate in interpreting. It invites the dialogue a catechism format usually forecloses; it invites its addressees to construct its meaning in their world by playing with its characters, dialoguing with Jesus, letting its images interact with the stuff of the hearers' own lives and world. Rebecca Chopp names this playing the logic of *abduction,* which readers employ to ask where the Gospel story *leads from* here and what present readers can *take from* its world to construct inclusive Christian communities today.[19] The final silence of the first Gospel creates space for intergenerational dialogue; its rhetoric of address is a model for contemporary catechesis.

CHAPTER 10

Emancipatory Dialogue
with Tradition

❦

For saying that . . . . (Mark 7:29)

HOW SHOULD WOMEN RECEIVE a Gospel and history of interpretation that largely excludes them? Some have left Christianity behind. Others have articulated feminist principles of interpretation to emancipate the good news from androcentric language and male bias. Mark's story of the Syrophoenician woman (7:24–30) offers a model of emancipatory dialogue with tradition. In this encounter Jesus, whose voice is the voice of authoritative teaching in this narrative, makes an offensive statement. He insists his mission is only to Jews and refers to the Gentile woman and her daughter as dogs, a derogatory Jewish term for Gentiles. In the face of authority speaking prejudice, the woman models emancipatory dialogue. She counters Jesus' closed word with a transformative word from her own experience and social location outside the boundaries of Jewish society. She speaks the truth of her experience in her Gentile household, where dogs have a place and eat the crumbs children let fall beneath the table. She models an active, transformative receiving of the gospel that emancipates its word from socially and culturally constructed biases and boundaries. The Syrophoenician woman's words and the three women's question in Mark 16:3, "Who will roll away the stone for us?" are the only two times the omniscient narrator gives women characters in Mark speaking parts.[1] The Syrophoenician woman speaks the truth of her experience to authority. Galatians 3:28 envisions a oneness in Christ in

108

which there is neither Jew nor Gentile, slave nor free, male and female. Mark 7:24–30 shows the first Christians confronting the social boundary between Jews and Gentiles. Feminist biblical hermeneutics was born among Christians who successfully abolished slavery nineteen centuries later and who struggle now to end other socially constructed dominations.

Mark 7:24 sets the scene between the Syrophoenician woman and Jesus geographically in the Gentile territory of Tyre and Sidon and theologically in secrecy and hiddenness. Jesus enters a house and wants no one to know he is there. This desire for concealment contradicts Jesus' teaching that a lamp belongs on a lampstand (4:21) and anything hidden will be revealed (4:22). The hiddenness is an instance of the silence and secrecy motif throughout Mark's Gospel. Despite Jesus' wish for secrecy, the Syrophoenician woman hears about him (7:24) and becomes in the story a model of hearing that yields a hundredfold (4:13–20). She seeks Jesus out, falls at his feet, and asks him to cast a demon from her daughter. The daughter gives the story an intergenerational setting.

The story begins as a typical miracle story. A suppliant comes to Jesus and requests healing (7:25–26). It ends typically, confirming that the girl has been set free of the demon (7:29–30). In the middle the story is atypical. Jesus refuses the mother's request. Only because of the words this Gentile mother speaks to counter Jesus' refusal does he free her daughter (7:29). This emancipation of a daughter's spirit takes place through a dialogue that forms the heart of this story and a turning point in the larger section of Mark's Gospel that stands between its double feeding miracles (6:34–44 and 8:1–10).

At first Jesus is mild in refusing the Syrophoenician woman's plea to cast the demon out of her daughter. He says, "Let the children be fed first," a unexpected response in which he gives priority to Jews in his mission but does not exclude the Gentile woman's daughter from his freeing power. But the comment proves a prelude to exclusion. He continues, "It is not fair to take the children's food and throw it to the dogs." These are fighting words. Jesus not only refuses to respond to the woman's request but insults her, putting her daughter and her down as Gentile dogs. His voice expresses boundaries and ethnic superiority.

However, the conversation is not over. The woman receives Jesus' word actively and transforms its meaning out of her experience as a Gentile woman—from her social location outside the margins. She addresses Jesus as Lord, which suggests that Jesus in this scene represents not his own point of view in history but the social location of the early church, in which believers disagreed about welcoming Gentiles. In Mark 7:28 the woman counters Jesus' refusal, "Lord, even the dogs under the table eat the children's crumbs." She stands the ground of her experience. Her rhetoric demonstrates how personal speech can create tension with oppressive social assumptions and redescribe reality. Dogs have a place in her household and eat the children's crumbs. She funds the word *dog* with its meaning in her social location.

Jewish law considered dogs unclean, probably because they ate dead things, which the law classifies as unclean. Unlike Jews, Gentiles let dogs into their houses. The Greek word for *dog* in the story is *kynaria*, which indicates small house dogs or lap dogs rather than dogs of the farm or streets.[2] Since Jewish law considered both Gentiles and dogs unclean, *dog* made a ready name for Gentiles. In the woman's household, bread for children inevitably results in crumbs under the table for the housedogs. She refuses to have the word *dog* place her daughter outside the boundaries of Jesus' power; in fact, she insists that dogs thrive on children's leftovers. The Syrophoenician woman turns a metaphor of exclusion—bread for the children—into a metaphor of inclusion, crumbs for the dogs.[3]

The Syrophoenician woman emancipates the prejudiced Jewish metaphor for Gentiles. From the woman's point of view, dogs have a place with children in her household. Her experience creates a contrary assertion that dogs are insiders like children. She sees similarity between dogs and children where Jesus, from a Jewish social context, sees only difference. Her word transforms the oppressive image and redescribes Christian community. Long-standing religious boundaries between Jews and Gentiles hold God's promise hostage in Jesus' statement. What emancipates the prejudice is the woman's refusal to accept the status Jesus' insult assigns her. She talks back to the voice of authority. She revalues the term *dog* by funding it with her own experience.

The context of this story within the Markan narrative is significant, for more is at stake in Jesus' anti-Gentile rhetoric than one woman's daughter. This scene stands at midpoint in a chiastic composition (see figure 12) that develops between the two feeding miracles—the first (A) on the Galilee, Jewish side of the Sea of Galilee (6:34–44); the second (A') on the Decapolis, Gentile side (8:1–10). The chiasm includes within the frame of the feeding miracles two healing miracles and two stories about liberating boundaries.[4]

The first three scenes within the frame of the two feeding stories take place in Jewish territory, the second three in Gentile territory. At the center of this chiasm two controversies face off. First, Jesus, some Pharisees, and his disciples argue about what is clean and unclean (7:1–23, C in the schema below). In juxtaposition to this story, Jesus and the Syrophoenician woman dialogue about whom he will feed and free (C'). The chiasm is about feeding, healing, and freeing Jews and freeing, healing, and feeding Gentiles. Schematically it looks like this:

Figure 12

A 6:34–44 Jesus feeds 5,000 on the Galilee side of the lake; twelve baskets of fragments.

B 6:53–56 Everyone who touches Jesus is healed at Gennesaret.

C 7:1–23 Jesus declares all food clean; evil comes not from what one puts in one's mouth but from what comes out of one's mouth.

C' 7:24–30 Syrophoenician woman in Tyre speaks her word that frees her daughter of a demon.

B' 7:31–37 Jesus heals a deaf-mute in the Decapolis region. He and his friends proclaim his healing in inverse proportion to Jesus urging them to keep it secret.

A' 8:1–10 Jesus feeds 4,000 Gentiles in the Decapolis area; seven baskets of fragments left over.

Geographical, theological, and intergenerational boundaries are at issue in this chiasm. In Mark 7:1–23, Pharisees accuse Jesus' disciples of eating with unclean hands and failing to observe other traditional washings. In response to the Pharisees, who wash but won't eat the food Jesus gives, Jesus explains to the crowd and subsequently to his disciples, "There is nothing outside a person that by going in can defile but the things that come out are what defiles" (7:15, 18, 20). Nonetheless, what comes out of Jesus' mouth in the next scene are words of exclusion and put-down when he enters Gentile territory and the Syrophoenician woman searches him out. The Jesus who had just rendered all foods clean in his dialogue with the Pharisees (7:19) vanishes; the Jesus of Mark 7:24–30 takes up the law-observant voice he has just silenced, enforcing boundaries and purveying exclusionary platitudes. He excludes the Gentiles from the abundant food and healing he brought to Jews in A and B.

The liberating word in the chiasm, its turning point, comes in the woman's speaking the truth of her own experience and social location, which stands outside the boundary of Jewish life. In her Gentile household, the dogs have a place and eat the crumbs children drop on the floor. From her emancipatory proclamation proceeds a Gentile mission that frees her daughter and a new generation for God's promises, frees a man who is mute to proclaim the power of Jesus' healing, and feeds a Gentile multitude. The woman who hears about Jesus transforms the crumbs her children drop beneath her table into an abundant and emancipatory word for the nations.

Crumbs as a metaphor do not suggest equal access to Jesus' power for Gentiles. However, two conversations appending the chiasm transform the image of crumbs into an image of abundance. At the end of the first Markan feeding miracle in 6:34–44, Jesus' disciples gather up twelve baskets of leftovers (*klasmata*) from the five loaves and two fish Jesus blesses, breaks, and gives to the disciples for the crowd. This is a huge quantity of crumbs. From the second feeding (Mark 8:1–10) on the Gentile side of the Sea of Galilee, Jesus' disciples gather up seven baskets of leftovers (*klasmata*) from seven loaves and a few fish. By including dogs with her children among those she feeds in her household, the Syrophoenician woman projects a Gentile household as a vision of Christian community and emancipates Jesus' mission from the religious barriers between Jews and Gentiles. Jesus' disciples don't understand, as the woman does, the abundant availability of God's power. In 8:17–21, following the second feeding in Mark's narrative, Jesus sets his disciples to worrying a third time about having enough bread, when he warns them against the leaven of the Pharisees. Immediately they remember they have only one loaf of bread with them. "Do you still not perceive or understand?" Jesus questions. In 8:19–21, he reviews the obvious mathematics of the abundant leftovers of the two feedings:

> "Do you not remember? When I broke the five loaves for the five thousand, how many baskets full of pieces did you collect?" They said to him, "Twelve." "And the seven for the four thousand, how many baskets full of broken pieces did you collect?" And they said to him, "Seven." Then he said to them, "Do you not yet understand?"

This rhetorical question silences the story characters and invites readers and hearers to interpret the twelve (the number of the tribes of Israel) baskets of leftovers from the Galilee feeding miracle and the seven (a number of completion) from the Gentile feeding.

The Syrophoenician woman's concern for her daughter places her story in an intergenerational context. In refusing to help this mother, Jesus appears bound to Jewish legal tradition. The narrative makes Jesus, the story character, religiously observant and prejudiced against Gentiles. Such a prejudice expressed in Jesus' voice suggests that the fearful, mute community of 70 C.E., for whom the first Gospel was written, also faces boundary issues between Jews and Gentiles. Such a social context makes Mark 7:24–30 an emancipatory dialogue with the world ahead of the text. The Syrophoenician woman teaches the Teacher; she speaks out of her doubly marginal experience as mother/woman and Gentile to alter the voice of authority. Her word frees her daughter and opens a future for her within the Christian community. The woman's word reimagines the Christian community as a household in which Jews and Gentiles share bread. Her word offers a catechetical model for calling people's own truth claims into dialogue with the gospel and the authoritative voices that interpret it.

Feminist hermeneutics of liberation recognizes cultural invisibility as an oppression; however, the Syrophoenician woman's social location is also, as bell hooks terms her social location, a homeplace[5] that sustains an emancipatory word. Feminist hermeneutics of liberation recognizes each person as a subject who perceives and constructs reality. Psycho- and linguistic analysis recognizes humans at work constructing their worlds out of their experience. In the Syrophoenician woman's story Mark's Gospel points to dialogue as potential space where people can entertain one another's truth claims, deconstruct oppressive social reality, and construct inclusive Christian community. David Tracy recommends conversation for this purpose and defines it as play, in which one can get caught up beyond oneself.[6]

Like the ending of Mark's Gospel, catechesis must employ a rhetoric of address that puts readers today in dialogue with the Gospel and in conversation with one another. Like the story of the Syrophoenician woman, catechesis must invite people to speak their own truth claims and resist objectified meaning or oppressive biases that exclude them and their experience. Worship and catechesis must create potential space in which a new generation can dialogue with the gospel and emancipate its proclamation anew for the world.[7]

Conclusion

☙

T HE WOMEN'S CONCLUDING SILENCE in Mark 16:8 creates generative potential space between kerygmatic narrative and reader, space in which readers and hearers can respond. The empty tomb and the fear and silence of the last disciple characters surviving in the narrative bring the readers and hearers to their own thresholds of faith, to the limit of words to speak the unspeakable, to the limit of story to make the absent One convincingly present, and to the limit of human experience to trust Who or What is beyond death. The women's silence invites the reader to hear the disclosing harmonics earlier testimony in the narrative has sounded. In their silence, the readers' hearing of the good news begins. In his absence, faith in Jesus Christ, the Son of God, can still arise, heal, and free.

The interpretation in this book reads Mark 16:8 in an intergenerational context. It recognizes that heightened, numinous fear characterizes Jesus' first-generation, eyewitness disciples in Mark's Gospel narrative—both the women and the men. The women's fear brings to the final verse of the Gospel the same fear the men disciples experience in two sea crossings and which the women and men who follow Jesus to Jerusalem also feel (10:32). Rhetorical analysis assumes that for its first hearers, the women's fear and the reference in 16:7 to Jesus' earlier prophecy that the blow to the shepherd will cause his disciples to stumble (*skandalisthēsesthe*) and scatter (*diaskorpisthēsontai*) (14:27–28) are important. If the rhetoric of Mark's ending mirrors the audience it addresses, the first Gospel addresses Christians who are faithful, yet fearful, scattered, stumbling, feeling both Jesus' absence and the silence of the eyewitnesses formerly

114

among them. In the space between the eyewitness generation of Jesus' disciples and the next generation, the rhetoric places three faithful, fearful women disciples, who as characters in the story point behind the text to eyewitnesses in history but primarily forward to the audience ahead of the text as silent foremothers to whom readers can give voice. The first Gospel hints that Peter, James, and John drink the martyrs' cup (10:38–39; 14:36, 38); the written text itself testifies that in the forty years between story time and writing time the women break their silence. The narrative suggests that, like the fear of the three faithful women at the empty tomb on Easter morning, the fear of the scattered, fearful disciples forty years later is not failed disbelief but a numinous threshold of commitment. In their silence in Mark 16:8b, the three women disciples are midwives of the birth of Jesus' word into story. Their silence is a rhetorical strategy that snips the history-like illusion the narrative creates and awaits a hearing of this new word in the audience ahead of the text. In our foremothers' silence, the narrative still calls the disciples of the next generation to speak for themselves and bring the gospel into dialogue with their lives.

Mary Magdalene Speaks

Hear in my silence
my voice as apostle
preacher of the story

See in the dark tomb
no angel from another world
but a young man in white

a believer from a new generation
who proclaims the Easter faith
in which every Christian arises
from the watery womb of baptism
there to set off on the road to the nations

there to live the message
my story still tells[1]

Notes

৩৬

Chapter 1
Invitation to Dialogue

1. This quotation and all quotations in English are from *The New Oxford Annotated Bible with the Apocryphal/Deuterocanonical Books*, New Revised Standard Version, ed. Bruce M. Metzger and Roland E. Murphy (New York: Oxford University Press, 1991); quotations in Greek are from the Nestle-Aland, *Novum Testamentum Graece*, 26th ed. (Stuttgart: Deutsche Bibelgesellschaft, 1987).

2. Rudolf Otto, *The Idea of the Holy*, 2nd ed., trans. John Harvey (New York: Oxford University Press, 1970); Mircea Eliade, *The Sacred and the Profane: The Nature of Religion*, trans. Willard R. Trask (New York: Harper & Row, 1957), 8–13.

3. Bruce M. Metzger, *A Textual Commentary on the Greek New Testament: A Companion Volume to the United Bible Societies' Greek New Testament* (London: United Bible Societies, 1971), 122–26. Metzger explains that the two oldest Greek manuscripts Sinaiticus (‭א‬) and Vaticanus (B), the Old Latin codex Bobiensis (it^k), the Sinaitic Syriac manuscript (sy^s), about one hundred Armenian manuscripts (arm^mss) and the two oldest Georgian manuscripts (written 897 and 913 C.E.) conclude the Gospel of Mark at 16:8, omitting vv. 9–20 or other variant endings. Clement of Alexandria and Origin show no knowledge of vv. 9–20, and Eusebius and Jerome "attest that the passage was absent from almost all Greek copies of Mark known to them." Internal evidence shows that the vocabulary and style of vv. 9–20 are non-Markan and the transition between v. 8 and v. 9 is awkward. Vocabulary and tone provide internal evidence against the originality of other variants as well. Metzger concludes after examining the documentary, external, and internal evidence that "the earliest ascertainable form of

the Gospel of Mark ended with 16.8." In note 7, Metzger acknowledges three possibilities concerning the ending: (a) the evangelist intended to close the Gospel at 16:8; (b) the Gospel was never finished; (c) the Gospel lost its last leaf accidentally before it was multiplied by transcription. Metzger favors the last possibility; this study favors the first, namely, that Mark 16:8 is the intended ending of the first Gospel. Further, *Novum Testamentum Graece* (26th ed., p. 147) identifies the following manuscripts and sources which omit vv. 9–20: א, B, 304 sy[s] sa[ms] arm[mss]; Cl, Or, Eus, Heir[ms]. *Novum Testamentum Graece* (27th ed.) also lists א, B, 304 sy[s] sa[ms] arm[mss] as sources omitting vv. 9–20.

4. Wilhelm Wrede, *The Messianic Secret*, trans. J. D. G. Greig (Greenwood, S.C.: Attic Press, 1971), 229. In this book, first published in 1901, Wrede argues that the messianic secret is a motif in Mark's Gospel that reveals the evangelist's hand as a theologian and disproves the evangelist's witness as a historian. In recognizing the secrecy motif as a deliberately composed, theological theme, Wrede shifts hermeneutical focus from the historical to the literary character of the Gospel, a primal nudge in a paradigm shift still in progress from historical to literary and linguistic criticism.

5. Claudia Setzer, "Excellent Women: Female Witnesses to the Resurrection," *Journal of Biblical Literature* 116, no. 2 (1997): 259–72.

6. Mary Ann Tolbert sees the named women disciples' response to the gospel as like the rocky ground in Mark's parable of the sower (4:1–20) in whom Jesus' word takes root but shrivels under persecution (*Sowing the Gospel: Mark's Gospel in Literary-Historical Perspective* [Minneapolis: Fortress Press, 1989], 295–97). In her view Mark puts the audience in the role of the ideal disciple.

7. Susan B. Matheson, *Dura-Europos* (New Haven: Yale University Art Gallery, 1982), 28. See also Clark Hopkins, *The Discovery of Dura-Europos*, ed. Bernard Goldman (New Haven: Yale University Press, 1979); M. Rostovtzeff, *Dura-Europos and Its Art* (Oxford: Clarendon Press, 1938); M. I. Rostovtzeff, ed., *Excavations at Dura-Europos: Preliminary Report of Fifth Season of Work, October 1931–March 1932* (New Haven: Yale University Press, 1934).

8. Barbara J. Mahar, "Actions of Boston Nun Raise Consciousness of Women's Ministries," *New Women, New Church* 23, no. 4 (Fairfax, Va.: Women's Ordination Conference, 2000), 1.

9. Mary Field Blenky, Blythe McVicker Clinchy, Nancy Rule Goldenberger, Jill Mattuck Tarule, *Women's Ways of Knowing: The Development of Self, Voice, and Mind* (New York: Basic Books, 1986), 23–34.

10. Pamela M. Fishman, "Interaction: The Work Women Do," in *Language, Gender, and Society*, ed. Barrie Thorne, Cheris Kramarae, and Nancy Henley (Rowley, Mass.: Newbury House, 1983), 89–101. Perhaps social relations have changed, making this study and the numerous others in this book out of date.

11. Sandra M. Schneiders, *With Oil in Their Lamps: Faith, Feminism, and the Future* (Mahwah, N.J.: Paulist Press, 2000), 4. This is Schneiders's proposal in the fifteenth Madeleva Lecture in Spirituality, named for Sister Madeleva Wolff,

longtime president of St. Mary's College, Notre Dame, Indiana, who established a theology school for women in 1954.

12. Anice Schervish, "The Cardinal Listened, Our Words Were Heard," *New Women, New Church* 23, no. 4 (Fairfax, Va.: Women's Ordination Conference, 2000), 4.

13. Chapter 9 will explore D. W. Winnicott's analysis of potential or transitional space. From the point of view of psychology and faith development, the empty tomb and the women's silence create transitional space, the space between the inside reality of our experience and the outside social world of all others, including God, the ultimate, ineffable Other. See Ann Belford Ulanov, *Finding Space: Winnicott, God, and Psychic Reality* (Louisville: Westminster John Knox Press, 2001), 115–16.

14. Denis Edwards, *Jesus the Wisdom of God: An Ecological Theology* (Maryknoll, N.Y.: Orbis Books, 1995), 42–43; Sharon Ringe, *Wisdom's Friends: Community and Christology in the Fourth Gospel* (Louisville: Westminster John Knox Press, 1999), 46–52.

15. For elaboration of her four feminist principles of feminist hermeneutics, see Elisabeth Schüssler Fiorenza, *Bread Not Stone: The Challenge of Feminist Biblical Interpretation* (Boston: Beacon Press, 1984), 15–22. For a description of her feminist pedagogy, see Elisabeth Schüssler Fiorenza, *But She Said: Feminist Practices of Biblical Interpretation* (Boston: Beacon Press, 1992), 186–88.

16. Elizabeth Struthers Malbon, *In the Company of Jesus: Characters in Mark's Gospel* (Louisville: Westminster John Knox Press, 2000), 189–225. In chapter 7, "The Major Importance of Minor Characters in Mark," Struthers Malbon terms these anonymous suppliants "exemplary." See also David Rhoads and Donald Michie, *Mark as Story: An Introduction to the Narrative of the Gospels* (Philadelphia: Fortress Press, 1982), 129.

Chapter 2
History Becomes Story

1. Elisabeth Schüssler Fiorenza, *In Memory of Her: A Feminist Theological Reconstruction of Christian Origins* (New York: Crossroad, 1985), 321–23. The women flee the tomb, not their commission to tell the disciples.

2. For a discussion about the dating of Mark's Gospel, see Werner Georg Kümmel, *Introduction to the New Testament,* trans. Howard Clark Kee (Nashville: Abingdon Press, 1986), 97–98; he places the writing of Mark about 70 C.E. with references to sources for various positions. Donald Senior places the writing of Mark's Gospel in Rome prior to the fall of the temple in 68–69 C.E. ("With Sword and Clubs," *Biblical Theology Bulletin* 17 [1987]: 10–20). He argues from its critique of abusive Roman authority evident in Nero's persecutions. Helmut Koester leans toward Syrian origins for the Gospel of Mark with the catastrophe of the Jewish War as a probable catalyst for its writing (*Introduc-*

tion to the New Testament, Vol. 2, *History and Literature of Early Christianity* [New York: Walter de Gruyter, 1982], 166–67).

3. Thomas E. Boomershine and Gilbert L. Bartholomew ("The Narrative Technique of Mark 16:8," *Journal of Biblical Literature* 100, no. 2 [1981]: 213–14 n. 4) refer to the following discussions of "*ephobounto gar*": C. H. Fraeling, "A Philological Note on Mark 16:8," *Journal of Biblical Literature* 34 (1915): 357–58; H. J. Cadbury, "Mark 16:8," *Journal of Biblical Literature* 34 (1915): 344–45; R. R. Ottley, "ephobounto gar," *Journal of Theological Studies* 27 (1926): 407–9; sentences ending in *gar* in Homer, Aeschylus, Euripedes, and Septuagint, W. Bauer, *Greek-English Lexicon of the New Testament and Other Early Christian Literature,* 2nd ed. (Chicago: University of Chicago Press, 1979), 151. See also Norman Perrin, *The Resurrection According to Matthew, Mark, and Luke* (Philadelphia: Fortress Press, 1977), 17.

4. Boomershine and Bartholomew, "Narrative Technique," 222.

5. Robert M. Fowler, *Let the Reader Understand: Reader-Response Criticism and Gospel of Mark* (Minneapolis: Augsburg-Fortress, 1991), 93–95.

6. Fowler, *Let the Reader,* 84. See also Boomershine and Bartholomew ("Narrative Technique," 221 n. 24), who cite Acts 8:26–40 and Augustine's *Confessions* 6.3. Mary Ann Tolbert cites Aristotle and Quintilian as ancient sources that consider the written text an aural medium (*Sowing the Gospel: Mark's World in Literary-Historical Perspective* [Minneapolis: Fortress Press, 1989], 44 n. 36).

7. John R. Donahue suggests that Jesus' silence before his accusers was a tradition prior to Mark, generated by Isa 53:7, "Yet he opened not his mouth" (*Are You the Christ? The Trial Narrative in the Gospel of Mark,* Society of Biblical Literature Dissertation Series 10 [Missoula, Mont.: Scholars Press, 1973], 86–87).

8. Donald H. Juel, *Messiah and Temple: The Trial of Jesus in the Gospel of Mark,* Society of Biblical Literature Dissertation Series 31 (Missoula, Mont.: Scholars Press, 1977), 46.

9. Seymour Chatman, *Story and Discourse: Narrative Structures in Fiction and Film* (Ithaca, N.Y.: Cornell University Press, 1978), 19.

10. Juel, *Messiah,* 55.

11. Patrick Keifert analyzes how Mark's Gospel references to history, within itself as a story, and to the audience ahead of the text ("Meaning and Reference: The Interpretation of Verisimilitude and the Gospel of Mark" [Th.D. diss., University of Chicago, 1982]). He draws on Paul Ricoeur to analyze the distance between speaking and writing, and speaking and encoding in a genre. See also Patrick Keifert, "Mind Reader and Maestro: Models for Understanding Biblical Interpreters," in *A Guide to Contemporary Hermeneutics: Major Trends in Biblical Interpretation,* ed. Donald K. McKim (Grand Rapids: Eerdmans, 1986), 222–28.

12. Paul Ricoeur, *Interpretation Theory: Discourse and the Surplus of Meaning* (Fort Worth: Texas Christian University Press, 1976), 16.

13. Keifert, "Meaning," 37.

14. Willem S. Vorster, "Meaning and Reference: The Parables of Jesus in

Mark 4," in *Text and Reality: Aspects of Reference in Biblical Texts* (Philadelphia: Fortress Press, 1985), 60.

15. For a discussion of the role of the beloved disciple in the Gospel of John, see R. Alan Culpepper, *Anatomy of the Fourth Gospel: A Study in Literary Design* (Philadelphia: Fortress Press, 1983), 42–49. See also Sandra M. Schneiders, *Written That You May Believe* (New York: Crossroad, 1998), chapter 14. She resists identifying the beloved disciple with John.

16. Norman Perrin, *The Resurrection According to Matthew, Mark, and Luke* (Philadelphia: Fortress Press, 1977), 19–24.

Chapter 3
Feminist Suspicion

1. See Elisabeth Schüssler Fiorenza's foundational work on feminist hermeneutics: *In Memory of Her: A Feminist Theological Reconstruction of Christian Origins* (New York: Crossroad, 1985); see also *Bread Not Stone: The Challenge of Feminist Biblical Interpretation* (Boston: Beacon Press, 1984).

2. Among the forty-five first- and third-world women who participated in the 1994 International Dialogue of Women Theologians on Violence against Women, a very basic hermeneutical principle emerged: "Whatever is good and life-giving for marginalized and excluded women is good for all." See Mary John Mananzan, Mercy Amba Oduyoye, Elsa Tamez, J. Shannon Clarkson, Mary C. Grey, Letty M. Russell, eds., *Women Resisting Violence: Spirituality for Life* (Maryknoll, N.Y.: Orbis Books, 1996), 182. This dialogue was called by the Women's Commission of the Ecumenical Association of Third World Theologians, formed in 1983 by the women members who took part in the Sixth Conference of EATWOT in Geneva in 1983. A preference for the poor, one of the principles of Catholic social teaching, is a preference for women, who with their children predominate among the poor.

3. Hans-Georg Gadamer, *Truth and Method*, 2nd rev. ed. (New York: Crossroad, 1989), 304.

4. Josephine Donovan, *Feminist Theory: The Intellectual Tradition of American Feminism* (New York: Fredrick Ungar, 1986); see chapter 1, "Enlightenment Liberal Feminism" (pp. 1–30).

5. Elizabeth Cady Stanton, *The Woman's Bible*, reprint ed. (New York: Arno Press, 1972). Cady Stanton gathered together a committee of twenty-three women who selected and commented upon Old and New Testament passages pertaining to women in the *The Woman's Bible Parts I, II* (New York: European Publishing Company, 1895, 1898). For a contemporary discussion of *The Woman's Bible,* see Schüssler Fiorenza, *In Memory of Her*, 7–14. For a critique of scholars' ambiguous reception of *The Woman's Bible* today, see Elisabeth Schüssler Fiorenza, *Sharing Her Word: Feminist Biblical Interpretation in Context* (Boston: Beacon Press, 1998), 59–71.

6. Cady Stanton, *Woman's Bible*, 8–9.

7. Ibid., 8.

8. Paul Ricoeur, *Freud and Philosophy: An Essay on Interpretation* (New Haven: Yale University Press, 1970), 32–36. See also Donovan, "Feminism and Marxism" and "Feminism and Freudianism" in *Feminist Theory*, 65–116. For a discussion of Ricoeur's hermeneutics of suspicion, see David Tracy, *Plurality and Ambiguity: Hermeneutics, Religion, and Hope* (San Francisco: Harper & Row, 1987), 73–80, who recognizes that the self must suspect systemic distortion not only in history but in the self. "The split self of postmodernity is caught between conscious activity and a growing realization of the radical otherness not only around but within us. We name that otherness, after all, the unconscious . . ." (p. 77).

9. Ricoeur, *Freud*, 26.

10. Ibid., 27–28. Ricoeur terms this responsiveness a second naiveté.

11. Simone de Beauvoir, *The Second Sex* (New York: Bantam Books, 1961), xi–xvii.

12. Judith Plaskow, *Standing Again at Sinai: Judaism from a Feminist Perspective* (San Francisco: Harper & Row, 1990), x. Plaskow reports a left-wing Orthodox rabbi telling a story that raised the question, "Are you a feminist or a Jew?" In the Bialystok Ghetto women wanted to rebel against the Nazis and join the Partisans, using guns they had smuggled into the ghetto. The women surrendered at the insistence of the men because they were Jews first and women second and had to stand in solidarity with their men. Jacqueline Grant records this same call to solidarity with black men for black women in *White Women's Christ and Black Women's Jesus: Feminist Christology and Womanist Response* (Atlanta: Scholars Press, 1989).

13. Kwok Pui-lan, "Racism and Ethnocentrism in Feminist Biblical Interpretation," in *Searching the Scriptures,* vol. 1, *A Feminist Introduction*, ed. Elisabeth Schüssler Fiorenza (New York: Crossroad, 1993), 104. See also Kwok Pui-lan, "Discovering the Bible in a Non-Biblical World," in *Lift Every Voice: Constructing Christian Theologies from the Underside*, ed. Susan Brooks Thistlethwaite and Mary Potter Engel (San Francisco: HarperCollins, 1998), 270–82.

14. Gadamer, *Truth and Method*, 301.

15. Elisabeth Schüssler Fiorenza, *Bread Not Stone*, 17. The use of male pronouns and such words as *man* and *mankind* makes women invisible in the language and marginalizes them in history and discourse.

16. Schüssler Fiorenza, *In Memory of Her*, 45.

17. Schüssler Fiorenza, *Bread Not Stone,* 5.

18. Elisabeth Schüssler Fiorenza, *But She Said: Feminist Practices of Biblical Interpretation* (Boston: Beacon Press, 1992), 115.

19. Ibid., 115 n. 29.

20. *New Oxford Annotated Bible with the Apocryphal/Deuterocanonical Books*, New Revised Standard Version, ed. Bruce M. Metzger and Roland E. Murphy (New York: Oxford University Press, 1991).

21. *Good News Bible With Deuterocanonicals/Apocrypha* (New York: American Bible Society, 1976).

22. *New American Bible*, St. Joseph Edition (New York: Catholic Book Publishing Company, 1970).

23. Paul Alan Mirecki concludes in his form-critical, redaction-critical, and literary-critical study that the longer ending of Mark is carefully composed ("Mark 16.9–20: Composition, Tradition and Redaction" [Th.D. diss., Harvard Divinity School, 1986], 150).

24. Rita Nakashima Brock, *Journeys by Heart: A Christology of Erotic Power* (New York: Crossroad, 1995), 76.

25. Ibid., 77.

26. Robert M. Fowler, *Let the Reader Understand: Reader-Response Criticism and the Gospel of Mark* (Minneapolis: Augsburg-Fortress, 1991), 66.

27. C. F. D. Moule, "St. Mark XVI.8 Once More," *New Testament Studies* 2 (1955): 58–59.

28. *Nag Hammadi Library in English*, ed. James M. Robinson (San Francisco: Harper & Row, 1978).

29. "Gospel of Thomas," trans. Helmut Koester and Thomas O. Lambdin, in *Nag Hammadi Library in English*, ed. James M. Robinson (San Francisco: Harper & Row, 1978), 118–30, logia 21, 61.

30. Antti Marjanen, *The Woman Jesus Loved: Mary Magdalene in the Nag Hammadi Library and Related Documents* (New York: Brill, 1996), 38. See also Susan Haskins, *Mary Magdalen: Myth and Metaphor* (New York: Riverhead Books, 1993), 35 n. 26.

31. Marjanen, *The Woman Jesus Loved*, 48–51.

32. Ibid., 48. Besides Thecla (*Acts of Paul and Thecla* 25.40), Marjanen also suggests as examples Mygdonia (*Acts of Thomas* 114), Charitine (*Acts of Philip* 44), and perhaps Maximilla (*Acts of Andrew* 9).

33. Schüssler Fiorenza, *In Memory of Her*, 90. See also Dennis Ronald MacDonald, *The Legend and the Apostle: The Battle for Paul in Story and Canon* (Philadelphia: Westminster Press, 1983), 17–23, 51–53, 90–96.

34. Ibid., 49–50. For Marjanen's third line of interpretation, see Marvin W. Meyer, "Making Mary Male: The Categories 'male' and 'female' in the Gospel of Thomas," *New Testament Studies* 31 (1985): 554–70.

35. Marjanen, *The Woman Jesus Loved*, 50–51.

36. Pheme Perkins, "The Gospel of Thomas," in *Searching the Scriptures,* vol. 2, *A Feminist Commentary* (New York: Crossroad, 1994), 558.

37. Haskins, *Mary Magdalen*, 37. See also Hans-Martin Schenke, "The Function and Background of the Beloved Disciple in the Gospel of John," in *Nag Hammadi Gnosticism and Early Christianity*, ed. Charles W. Hedrick and Robert Hodgson, Jr. (Peabody, Mass.: Hendrickson, 1986), 122. Schenke recognizes that, like the *Gospel of Mary*, the *Gospel of Philip* portrays Mary Magdalene as a beloved disciple.

38. Elaine Pagels, *The Gnostic Gospels* (New York: Vantage Books, 1981), 16.

39. Ibid., 32.

40. Karen L. King, "The Gospel of Mary Magdalene," in *Searching the Scriptures*, vol. 2, *A Feminist Commentary* (New York: Crossroad, 1994), 621.

41. Ibid., 623–24.

42. Haskins, *Mary Magdalen*, 35.

43. Roman Missal, *Lectionary for Mass: Book of Gospels*, New American Bible (NAB) (New York: Catholic Book Publishing Company, 1984), 195–96.

44. Constitution on the Sacred Liturgy (*Sacrosanctum Concilium*), in *Documents of Vatican II*, ed. Walter M. Abbott, S.J. (New York: America Press, 1966), §51.

45. One wonders what is at stake in this omission. Doesn't such an omission continue to prostitute Mary Magdalene's memory as Jesus' disciple, the first witness of the resurrection, and the apostle to the other apostles. The hymn "In the Garden," based on John 20, including John 20:10–18, is popular at funerals, a use that makes Mary Magdalene's meeting the risen Jesus a parallel for Jesus meeting the beloved Christian at death.

46. Schüssler Fiorenza, *In Memory of Her*, xiii–xiv.

Chapter 4
Liberating Reading

1. Elisabeth Schüssler Fiorenza, "The Ethics of Biblical Interpretation: Decentering Biblical Scholarship," *Journal of Biblical Literature* 107, no. 1 (1988): 5. In this, her presidential address to the Society of Biblical Literature, Schüssler Fiorenza says, "One's social location or rhetorical context is decisive of how one sees the world, constructs reality, or interpets biblical texts."

2. Elisabeth Schüssler Fiorenza, *In Memory of Her: A Feminist Theological Reconstruction of Christian Origins* (New York: Crossroad, 1985), xx, 86 n. 51.

3. Ibid., 84–85.

4. Ibid., 30–31.

5. Ibid., 56.

6. Ibid., 86–90.

7. Ibid., 56.

8. Ibid., 32–33.

9. Ibid., 205–41.

10. Ibid., 322–23. Schüssler Fiorenza draws on Luise Schottroff's reading of Mark 16:8 in "Maria Magdalena um die Frauen am Grabe Jesu," *Evangelische Theologie* 42 (1982): 21.

11. Sandra M. Schneiders, *The Revelatory Text: Interpreting the New Testament as Sacred Scripture* (San Francisco: HarperSanFrancisco, 1991). This book explores how the Gospel narratives refer to history behind the text, the narrative world within the text, and the audience in front of the text.

12. Rebecca S. Chopp, *Saving Work: Feminist Practices in Theological Education* (Louisville: Westminster John Knox Press, 1995), 36–37. See also Elisabeth Schüssler Fiorenza, "The Politics of Otherness: Biblical Interpretation as a Critical Praxis of Liberation," in *Expanding the View: Gustavo Gutiérrez and the Future of Liberation Theology*, ed. Marc H. Ellis and Otto Jadura (Maryknoll, N.Y.: Orbis Books, 1988), 315–18.

13. Marie Theres Wacker, "Part One: Historical, Hermeneutical, and Methodological Foundations," in *Feminist Interpretations: The Bible in Women's Perspective* (Minneapolis: Fortress Press, 1998), 71–73. Mieke Bal critiques the embeddedness of male perspective in metaphor in "Metaphors He Lives By," *Semeia* 61 (1993): 185–207. For Bal's analysis in action, see Cheryl Exum, *Fragmented Women: (Sub)versions of Biblical Narrative*, Journal for the Study of the Old Testament Supplement 163 (Sheffield: Sheffield Academic Press, 1996).

14. Karen L. King, "Canonization and Marginalization: Mary of Magdala," in *Women's Sacred Scriptures*, ed. Kwok Pui-lan and Elisabeth Schüssler Fiorenza, Concilium 1998/3 (Maryknoll, N.Y.: Orbis Books, 1998), 29–36.

15. Ibid., 31; see also Karen L. King, "The Gospel of Mary Magdalene," in *Searching the Scriptures,* vol. 2, *A Feminist Commentary*, ed. Elisabeth Schüssler Fiorenza (New York: Crossroad, 1994), 601–34.

16. Elaine Wainwright, *Shall We Look for Another? A Feminist Rereading of the Matthean Jesus* (Maryknoll, N.Y.: Orbis Books, 1998), 9.

17. Iris Marion Young, *Justice and the Politics of Difference* (Princeton: Princeton University Press, 1990), 43.

18. Judith Plaskow, *Standing Again at Sinai: Judaism from a Feminist Perspective* (San Francisco: HarperSanFrancisco, 1990), 2.

19. Ibid., 11–12. Plaskow identifies as common elements of women's experience "shared biological experience, common imposition of Otherness, exclusion from the encoding of cultural meanings."

20. Toinette Eugene, "Two Heads Are Better Than One," *Daughters of Sarah* (summer 1993): 9–11.

21. bell hooks, *Feminist Theory: From Margin to Center* (Boston: South End Press, 1984), Preface.

22. Young, *Politics of Difference*, 48–63. Young usefully distinguishes five faces of oppression: (1) exploitation—people disproportionately profiting from workers' labor; (2) marginalization—people not useful to the system; (3) powerlessness—people who take orders but rarely give them, who lack the authority, status, and sense of self professionals tend to have; (4) cultural imperialism—dominant groups and meanings render other groups and meanings invisible; (5) violence—systemic permission to practice violence.

23. Karen Baker-Fletcher, "Soprano Obligato: The Voices of Black Women and American Conflict in the Thought of Anna Julia Cooper," in *A Troubling in My Soul: Womanist Perspectives on Evil and Suffering*, ed. Emilie M. Townes (Maryknoll, N.Y.: Orbis Books, 1993), 183. See also Karen Baker-Fletcher, *Sis-*

ters of Dust, Sisters of Spirit: Womanist Wordings on God and Creation (Minneapolis: Fortress Press, 1998), 112.

24. bell hooks, *Yearning: Race, Gender, and Cultural Politics* (Boston: South End Press, 1990), 153. Katie Geneva Cannon, *Katie's Canon: Womanism and the Soul of the Black Community* (New York: Continuum, 1995).

25. Cannon, *Katie's Canon*, 161–70.

26. Rebecca S. Chopp, *The Power to Speak: Feminism, Language, God* (New York: Crossroad, 1989), 14.

27. Susan Brooks Thistlethwaite, *Sex, Race, and God: Christian Feminism Black and White* (New York: Crossroad, 1989), 58.

28. Young, *Politics of Difference*, 34; see also Chopp, *Saving Work*, 62–64.

29. David Tracy in *Plurality and Ambiguity: Hermeneutics, Religion, Hope* (Chicago: University of Chiacgo Press, 1987) writes: "The final indignity for anyone is to be forbidden one's own voice or to be robbed of one's own experience" (p. 106). He enjoins listening to the narratives of others, especially "others" who have had to suffer our otherness imposed on their interpretations of their own history and classics (p. 72).

30. Chopp describes the just person as one who hears others into speech and who "continually forms new possibilities of emancipatory transformation in community" (*Power to Speak*, 97).

31. Plaskow, *Standing*, 57.

32. Chopp, *Power to Speak*, 37–38. Chopp names the virtue of emancipatory community "vitality" or "creativity" (p. 97).

33. Ibid., 59–62.

34. Tracy (*Plurality and Ambiguity*, 9, 19 n. 29) explains that these statements are variations of the transcendental imperatives articulated by Bernard Lonergan: "Be attentive, be intelligent, be responsible, be loving, and if necessary, change" (Lonergan, *Method in Theology* [New York: Seabury, 1972], 231).

35. Chopp, *Power to Speak*, 97–98.

36. Tracy, *Plurality and Ambiguity*, 93.

37. Francis Schüssler Fiorenza, "The Crisis of Scriptural Authority: Interpretation and Reception," *Interpretation* 44, no. 4 (1990): 364.

Chapter 5
Women of Galilee

1. Rosalie Ryan argues that the Gospels use the word *akolouthein* exclusively to describe the act of becoming a disciple of Jesus ("Women from Galilee and Discipleship in Luke," *Biblical Theology Bulletin* 15 [1985]: 58–59). See also Elisabeth Schüssler Fiorenza (*In Memory of Her: A Feminist Theological Reconstruction of Christian Origins* [New York: Crossroad, 1985], 320), who agrees with Ryan, citing Mark's uses of the same verb to describe Simon and Andrew's response to Jesus' invitation to follow him (1:18): "And immediately they left

their nets and followed him (*ēkolouthēsan autǭ*)." Elizabeth Struthers Malbon ("Fallible Followers: Women and Men in the Gospel of Mark," in *The Bible and Feminist Hermeneutics*, ed. Mary Ann Tolbert, Semeia 28 [Chico, Calif.: Scholars Press, 1983], 41) cites Winsome Munro's cautious reading of the verb *akoloutheō*, which "always denotes commitment of some degree and never mere physical following when it is applied to Jesus." For a discussion of discipleship in Matthew, see Janice Capel Anderson, "Matthew: Gender and Reading," in *The Bible and Feminist Hermeneutics*, 18.

2. Luise Schottroff, "Maria Magdalena und die Frauen am Grabe Jesu," *Evangelische Theologie* 42 (1982): 13. The English is my translation of Schottroff's observation, "Auch dieses Satzchen zeigt erneut, dass Markus die Frauen unter dem Kreuz als die Repräsentanten der Jünger und ihrer Kreuzesnachfolge ansieht."

3. Elisabeth Schüssler Fiorenza, *In Memory of Her: A Feminist Theological Reconstruction of Christian Origins* (New York: Crossroad, 1985), 321. Ryan ("Women from Galilee," 57) argues that in Luke 8:38, 9:19, 22:56 "to be with Jesus" (*syn autǭ eimi*) is a similar technical expression for discipleship.

4. Luise Schottroff, *Lydia's Impatient Sisters: A Feminist Social History of Early Christianity* (Louisville: Westminster John Knox, 1995), 214.

5. Ibid., 205–14.

6. Schottroff, "Maria Madgalena," 11. The English is my translation of Schottroff's comment, "alle sind aller *diakonoi*. Diakonia hat also bei Markus einen viel umfassendernen Sinn als nur den Tischdienst: sie bezeichnet die Beziehung von Jüngern untereinander wie die Beziehung von Jüngern zu Jesus wie auch von Jesus zu den Menschen."

7. Ibid., 12. "der Begriff nahezu synonym mit *akolouthein*."

8. Monika Fander, *Die Stellung der Frau im Markusevangelium* (Altenberge: Telos Verlag, 1990), 34. The English is my translation of Fander's observations, "Innerhalb der exemplarischen Komposition des ersten Tages des Wirkens Jesu wird das Problem der Nachfolge anhand der vorbildlichen Reaktion einer Frau erläutert, zu der nicht nur die wundersüchtige Menge, sondern auch die Jünger in Kontrast stehen. Durch die Einfügung der Jüngernamen in 1,29 wird die Geschichte zu einer Jüngergeschichte, in der eine Frau nicht nur für den Leser, sondern auch für die Erstberufenen als Vorbild wahrer Nachfolge und wahren Jüngerseins dargestellt wird."

Chapter 6
Numinous Fear

1. J. Lee Magness finds the women's fear a heightened, numinous state, typical of the endings of miracle stories throughout the Gospel (*Sense and Absence: Structure and Suspension in the Ending of Mark's Gospel* [Atlanta: Scholars Press, 1986], 92–102). Andrew T. Lincoln sees the women's fear negatively, as the reason they fail to carry the good news of Jesus' resurrection to his male disciples

("The Promise and Failure: Mark 16.7–8," *Journal of Biblical Literature* 108, no. 2 [1989]: 283–300). Mary Ann Tolbert sees the female disciples like the male disciples as failures, rocky ground in whom the seed of the gospel cannot take deep root, and she sees the reader ahead of the text as the ideal disciple (*Sowing the Gospel: Mark's World in Literary-Historical Perspective* [Minneapolis: Fortress Press, 1989], 295–97).

2. Lincoln, "Promise and Failure," 287.

3. Tolbert, *Sowing the Gospel*, 295.

4. Magness, *Sense and Absence*, 92–102.

5. Robert M. Fowler, *Loaves and Fishes: The Function of the Feeding Miracles in the Gospel of Mark* (Chico, Calif.: Scholars Press, 1981), 113–16. The three sets of doublet stories function with the three passion predictions to create an interlocking narrative chain that extends from Mark 4:35 to 10:52.

6. John R. Donahue, *Are You the Christ? The Trial Narrative in the Gospel of Mark*, Society of Biblical Literature Dissertation Series 10 (Missoula, Mont.: Scholars Press, 1973), 58–59; see also chapter 1, nn. 58 and 59.

Chapter 7
Silence, Secrets, and Speech

1. J. Lee Magness, *Sense and Absence: Structure and Suspension in the Ending of Mark's Gospel* (Atlanta: Scholars Press, 1986) 88.

2. Donald H. Juel, *Messianic Exegesis: Christological Interpretation of the Old Testament in Early Christianity* (Philadelphia: Fortress Press, 1988), 171.

3. Elizabeth Struthers Malbon ("The Jewish Leaders in the Gospel of Mark: A Literary Study of Marcan Characterization," *Journal of Biblical Literature* 108, no. 2 [1989]: 277 n. 52) utilizes E. M. Forster's sense of "round" characters, those whose responses go beyond the stereotypical or representative and "exhibit multiple aspects of their relationship to Jesus: both faith and doubt, both trust and fear, both obedience and denial." See also Elizabeth Struthers Malbon, *In the Company of Jesus: Characters in Mark's Gospel* (Louisville: Westminster John Knox Press, 2000), 10–11, 223.

4. Mary Ann Tolbert asks, "If the women frustrate the hopes of the authorial audience for individuals to prove faithful to the courageous example of Jesus and follow his way by going out and sowing the word abroad, is there anyone else available to fulfill that task?" She answers, "Of course there is: the audience itself. By involving the audience in the narrative time of Jesus' life and death, by aligning their evaluative perspective with that of the narrator and Jesus, permitting them to share superior knowledge from the beginning of who Jesus was and what he was in the world to do, Mark has created in the role of the authorial audience the perfect disciple" (*Sowing the Gospel: Mark's World in Literary-Historical Perspective* [Minneapolis: Fortress Press, 1989], 297).

Chapter 8
Calling a New Generation

1. Werner H. Kelber, *The Oral and the Written Gospel* (Philadelphia: Fortress Press, 1983), 92.

2. Ibid., 208.

3. Ibid., 210–11.

4. Carla Ricci suggests in regard to Luke's Gospel that the sets of three witnesses meet the required minimum in Deuteronomy 19:15 for evidence to be valid (*Mary Magdalene and Many Others: Women Who Followed Jesus* [Minneapolis: Fortress Press, 1994], 127–29).

5. Raymond E. Brown and John P. Meier, *Antioch and Rome: New Testament Cradles of Catholic Christianity* (New York: Paulist Press, 1983), 194.

6. Ekkehard W. Stegemann hears in the phrase "the cup I drink" (*to potērion ho egō pinō*) a "Formulierung des Martyriumstodes" ("Zur Rolle von Petrus, Jakobus und Johannes im Markusevangelium," *Evangelische Theologie* 42 [1986]: 373).

7. Ibid., 374. The English is my translation of Stegemann's observations: "So aber fande die Auswahl von Petrus, Jakobus, und Johannes ihre Erklärung darin, ass sie die den Lesern bereits als Martyrer bekannten Jünger Jesu und damit Teilnehmer seines Geschicks im engeren Sinne geworden sind."

8. Eusebius, *Ecclesiastical History* 3.5.3.

9. Marla J. Selvidge, *Women, Cult, and Miracle Recital: A Redaction Critical Investigation of Mark 5.24-34* (Lewisburg: Bucknell University Press, 1990), 81.

10. Ibid., 87.

11. Ibid., 97.

12. Ibid., 105–6.

Chapter 9
Narrative and Reader

1. Julia Kristeva, "Word, Dialog, and Novel," in *Desire in Language: A Semiotic Approach to Literature and Art*, ed. Leon S. Roudiez, trans. Thomas Gora, Alice Jardine, Leon S. Roudiez (New York: Columbia University Press, 1980), 64–91.

2. Ibid., 74–76.

3. Rebecca S. Chopp, *The Power to Speak: Feminism, Language, God* (New York: Crossroad, 1989), 21–24.

4. D. W. Winnicott, *Playing and Reality* (London: Tavistock Publications, 1971), 14. Winnicott asserts that adding the intermediate area of human experiencing to the usual recognition of inner and outer reality makes a more adequate description of the human person.

5. Ibid., 14–15.

6. Ibid., 107–10. This section on "potential space" summarizes the argument of Winnicott's first chapter, "Transitional Objects and Transitional Phenomena" (pp. 1–25).

7. Ibid., 108.

8. Ann Belford Ulanov, *Finding Space: Winnicott, God, and Psychic Reality* (Louisville: Westminster John Knox Press, 2001) 115.

9. Ulanov, *Finding Space,* 141.

10. Kristeva, "Place Names," in *Desire in Language,* 283.

11. Ibid., 287.

12. Ibid., 291.

13. Ana-Maria Rizzuto, *The Birth of the Living God: A Psychoanalytic Study* (Chicago: University of Chicago Press, 1979), 177–211. In her conclusions Rizzuto explains, "Throughout life God remains a transitional object at the service of gaining leverage with oneself, with others, and with life itself. This is so, not because God is God, but because, like the teddy bear, he has obtained a good half of his stuffing from the primary objects the child has 'found' in his life. The other half of God's stuffing comes from the child's capacity to 'create' a God according to his needs" (p. 179). This image remains a potentially available representation for the continuous process of psychic integration (p. 180). All children in the Western world form at least a rudimentary God representation; it must "be revised to keep pace with changes in self-representation" or it becomes ridiculous, irrelevant, or dangerous (p. 200). She agrees with Winnicott: "The entire study suggests that Winnicott was accurate in locating religion—and God—in what he called transitional space. That is the space for illusion, where art, culture, and religion belong. This is the place where man's life finds the full relevance of his objects and meaning for himself" (p. 209).

14. *Sharing the Light of Faith: National Catechetical Directory for Catholics in the United States* (Washington, D.C.: U.S. Catholic Conference, 1979), §32. See also the *Catechism of the Catholic Church,* §3; *General Directory for Catechesis* (Washington, D.C.: U.S. Catholic Conference, 1998), §24.

15. Elisabeth Schüssler Fiorenza explains that her notion of the Bible as a formative root-model allows women "to reclaim the Bible as enabling resource, bread not stone, as legacy and heritage, not only of patriarchal religion but also of woman-church as a discipleship of equals" (*Bread Not Stone: The Challenge of Feminist Biblical Interpretation* [Boston: Beacon Press, 1984], xvii).

16. James B. Dunning, "Rite of Christian Initiation of Adults: Model of Adult Growth," *Worship* 53, no. 2 (1979): 142–56.

17. John Paul II, "Apostolic Constitution Fidei Depositum on the Publication of the *Catechism of the Catholic Church* Prepared Following the Second Vatican Council," in *Catechism of the Catholic Church* (New York: Catholic Book Publishing Co., 1994), 1.

18. Ibid., §11.

19. Chopp, *Power to Speak,* 37–38. We use the logic of induction when we

generalize from facts and the logic of deduction when we apply general principles to specific cases. Abduction is a third logic that recognizes the power of language, especially imagery, to connect with readers' experience and lead from the text to life.

Chapter 10
Emancipatory Dialogue with Tradition

1. Joanna Dewey, "Women in the Synoptic Gospels: Seen But Not Heard?" *Biblical Theology Bulletin* 27, no. 2 (1997): 59.

2. Walter Bauer, *A Greek-English Lexicon of the New Testament and Other Early Christian Literature,* trans. and adapted by William F. Arndt and F. Wilbur Gingrich (Chicago: University of Chicago Press, 1979), 457.

3. Paul Ricoeur, *The Rule of Metaphor: Multidisciplinary Studies of the Creation of Meaning in Language,* trans. Robert Czerny with Kathleen McLaughlin and John Costello, S.J. (Toronto: University of Toronto Press, 1977), 42. Paul Ricoeur analyzes how new metaphors redescribe reality. They employ the copulative verb *is* to set up a tension between *is* and *is not,* between similarity and difference (p. 247). Ricoeur sees the literal level of a metaphor as the *is not,* the determinative level, and the metaphoric level as the *is,* the level of a new assertion, of "ontological vehemence" and commitment to a redescription of reality (p. 255). The *is not* is the pole of a metaphor that is familiar; the *is* is the pole that is a new, strange description. The literal *is not* resists the metaphorical; the metaphorical *is* redescribes the literal. In "Metaphors He Lives By," *Semeia* 61 (1993): 205, Mieke Bal insists that metaphors often sublimate gender and other boundaries; she sees metaphor as "a key to an understanding of language—including itself—as a form of struggle."

4. Mark 6:45–52 is the second sea crossing, the closing frame of the chiasm that begins with the first sea crossing in 4:35–41. Mark interlocks the sea-crossing chiasm with the chiasm that the feeding miracles frame by telling the first feeding miracle in 6:30–44 immediately before the concluding see crossing.

5. bell hooks, *Yearning* (Boston: South End Press, 1990), 153; see chapter 5, "Homeplace: A Site of Resistance" (pp. 41–50).

6. David Tracy, *Plurality and Ambiguity: Hermeneutics, Religion, Hope* (Chicago: University of Chicago Press, 1987), 18–23.

7. For further support of this chapter's position, see Gerd Theissen, *The Gospels in Context: Social and Political History in the Synoptic Tradition* (Philadelphia: Fortress Press, 1991).

Epilogue
Mary Magdalene Speaks

1. The spice-bearing women are sentinels at the baptismal font as they are at the empty tomb in the final scene of the first Gospel. At Dura-Europos, the ear-

liest Christian house church that archaeologists have found, the three spice-bearing women guard the baptismal font in a fresco on the wall. The Orthodox Church celebrates a Sunday of the Spice-Bearing Women, the third Sunday after Easter. Dura-Europos is the Pompeii of the eastern frontier of the Roman empire, a treasury of art preserved when Roman soldiers reinforced the city walls by filling the houses closest to them with debris to form a defensive against invaders in 256 C.E. The three women on the way to Jesus' tomb carry torches in one hand and bowls of spices in the other. See Susan B. Matheson, *Dura-Europos* (New Haven: Yale University Art Gallery, 1982), 28; see also Clark Hopkins, *The Discovery of Dura-Europos*, trans. Bernard Goldman (New Haven: Yale University Press, 1979); M. Rostovtzeff, *Dura-Europos and Its Art* (Oxford: Oxford at the Clarendon, 1938); M. I. Rostovtzeff, ed., *Excavations at Dura-Europos: Preliminary Report of Fifth Season of Work, October 1931–March 1932* (New Haven: Yale University Press, 1934).

Bibliography

Abbott, Walter M., S.J., ed. *Documents of Vatican II.* New York: America Press, 1966.

Achtemeier, Paul J. *Mark.* Proclamation Commentaries. Philadelphia: Fortress Press, 1975.

Adam, Adolf. *The Liturgical Year: Its History and Its Meaning after the Reform of the Liturgy.* Translated by Matthew J. O'Connell. New York: Pueblo Publishing Company, 1981.

Alter, Robert. *The Art of Biblical Narrative.* New York: Basic Books, 1981.

Anderson, Janice Capel, and Stephen D. Moore, eds. *Mark and Method: New Approaches in Biblical Studies.* Minneapolis: Fortress Press, 1992.

Aquino, Maria Pilar. *Our Cry for Life: Feminist Theology from Latin America.* Translated by Dinah Livingston. Maryknoll, N.Y.: Orbis Books, 1993.

Auerbach, Erich. *Mimesis: The Representation of Reality in Western Literature.* Translated by Willard R. Trask. Princeton: Princeton University Press, 1953.

Baker-Fletcher, Karen. *A Singing Something: Womanist Reflection on Anna Julia Cooper,* 68–97. New York: Crossroad, 1994.

———. *Sisters of Dust, Sisters of Spirit: Womanist Wordings on God and Creation.* Minneapolis: Fortress Press, 1998.

———. "Soprano Obligato: The Voices of Black Women and American Conflict in the Thought of Anna Julia Cooper." In *A Troubling in My Soul: Womanist Perspectives on Evil and Suffering,* edited by Emilie M. Townes, 172–85. Maryknoll, N.Y.: Orbis Books, 1993.

Bal, Mieke. "Metaphors He Lives By." *Semeia* 61 (1993): 185–207.

Barta, Karen A. *The Gospel of Mark.* Wilmington, Del.: Michael Glazier, 1988.

Bauer, Walter. *A Greek-English Lexicon of the New Testament and Other Early*

Christian Literature. Translated and adapted by William F. Arndt and F. Wilbur Gingrich. Chicago: University of Chicago Press, 1979.

Beavis, Mary Ann. "From the Margin to the Way: A Feminist Reading of the Story of Bartimaeus." *Journal of Feminist Studies* 14, no. 1 (1998): 19–40.

———. *Mark's Audience: The Literary and Social Setting of Mark 4.11–12*. Journal for the Study of the New Testament Supplement Series 33. Sheffield: JSNT Press, 1989.

———. "Women As Models of Faith in Mark." *Biblical Theology Bulletin* 18 (1989): 3–9.

Beck, Robert R. *Nonviolent Story: Narrative Conflict Resolution in the Gospel of Mark*. Maryknoll, N.Y.: Orbis Books, 1996.

Benjamin, Jessica. *Bonds of Love: Psychoanalysis, Feminism, and the Problem of Domination*. New York: Pantheon Books, 1988.

Berman, Art. *From the New Criticism to Deconstruction: The Reception of Structuralism and Post-Structuralism*. Urbana: University of Illinois Press, 1988.

Best, Ernest. *Disciples and Discipleship: Studies in the Gospel according to Mark*. Edinburgh: T & T Clark, 1983.

———. *Following Jesus: Discipleship in the Gospel of Mark*. Sheffield: JSOT Press, 1981.

———. *Mark: The Gospel as Story*. Edinburgh: T & T Clark, 1986.

———. "Mark's Narrative Technique." *Journal for the Study of the New Testament* 37 (1989): 43–58.

Black, C. Clifton. *The Disciples According to Mark: Markan Redaction in Current Debate*. Journal for the Study of the Old Testament, Supplement Series 27. Sheffield: JSOT Press, 1989.

Blevins, James L. *The Messianic Secret in Markan Research 1901–1976*. Washington, D.C.: University Press of America, 1981.

Boomershine, Thomas E. "Mark 16:8 and the Apostolic Commission." *Journal of Biblical Literature* 100, no. 2 (1981): 225–39.

Boomershine, Thomas E., and Gilbert L. Bartholomew. "The Narrative Technique of Mark 16:8." *Journal of Biblical Literature* 100, no. 2 (1981): 213–23.

Booth, Wayne C. *The Rhetoric of Fiction*. Chicago: University of Chicago Press, 1961.

Breech, James. *Jesus and Postmodernism*. Minneapolis: Fortress Press, 1990.

———. *The Silence of Jesus: The Authentic Voice of the Historical Man*. Philadelphia: Fortress Press, 1983.

Brock, Rita Nakashima. *Journeys by Heart: A Christology of Erotic Power*. New York: Crossroad, 1995.

Brooten, Bernadette J. "Early Christian Women and Their Cultural Context: Issues of Method in Historical Reconstruction." In *Feminist Perspectives on Biblical Scholarship*, edited by Adela Yarbro Collins, 65–92. Chico, Calif.: Scholars Press, 1985.

———. "Jewish Women's History in the Roman Period: A Task for Christian

Theology." In *Christians Among Jews and Gentiles*, edited by George W. E. Nickelsburg and George W. MacRae, 22–30. Philadelphia: Fortress Press, 1977.

———. *Women Leaders in the Ancient Synagogue: Inscriptional Evidence and Background Issues*. Brown Judaic Studies 36. Chico, Calif.: Scholars Press, 1982.

Brown, Raymond E., S.S. *The Community of the Beloved Disciple*. Ramsey, N.J.: Paulist Press, 1979.

Brown, Raymond E., S.S., and John P. Meier. *Antioch and Rome: New Testament Cradles of Catholic Christianity*. New York: Paulist Press, 1983.

Bultmann, Rudolf. *The History of the Synoptic Tradition*. New York: Harper & Row, 1963.

Cannon, Katie Geneva. *Black Womanist Ethics*. American Academy of Religion Academy Series 60. Atlanta: Scholars Press, 1988.

———. *Katie's Canon: Womanism and the Soul of the Black Community*. New York: Continuum, 1995.

Cannon, Katie G., and Elisabeth Schüssler Fiorenza, eds. *Interpretation for Liberation*. Semeia 47. Atlanta: Scholars Press, 1989.

Chatman, Seymour. *Story and Discourse: Narrative Structure in Fiction and Film*. Ithaca, N.Y.: Cornell University Press, 1978.

Chopp, Rebecca S. *The Power to Speak: Feminism, Language, God*. New York: Crossroad, 1989.

———. *Saving Work: Feminist Practices in Theological Education*. Louisville: Westminster John Knox Press, 1995.

Christ, Carol P., and Judith Plaskow, eds. *Womanspirit Rising: A Feminist Reader in Religion*. San Francisco: Harper & Row, 1979.

Collins, Adela Yarbro, ed. *Feminist Perspectives on Biblical Scholarship*. Chico, Calif.: Scholars Press, 1985.

———. *The Beginning of the Gospel: Probings of Mark in Context*. Minneapolis: Fortress, 1992.

Collins, Raymond F. *Introduction to the New Testament*. Garden City, N.Y.: Doubleday, 1983.

Cook, Guillermo, and Ricardo Foulkes. *Marcos*. Commentario Biblico Hispano Americano. Miami: Editorial Caribe, 1990.

Crossan, John Dominic. "A Form for Absence: The Markan Creation of Gospel." In *Rhetoric, Eschatology, and Ethics in the New Testament*, edited by William Beardslee, 41–56. Semeia 12. Missoula, Mont.: Scholars Press, 1978.

Culpepper, R. Alan. *Anatomy of the Fourth Gospel: A Study in Literary Design*. Philadelphia: Fortress Press, 1983.

Dahl, Nils A. *The Crucified Messiah and Other Essays*. Minneapolis: Augsburg Press, 1974.

Davone, Paul. "The Characterization and Narrative Function of the Women at the Tomb (Mark 15.40–41, 47; 16,1–8)." *Biblica* 77 (1996): 375–97.

de Beauvoir, Simone. *The Second Sex.* Translated by H. M. Parshly. New York: Bantam Books, 1961.

Dewey, Joanna. "From Oral Stories to Written Text." In *Women's Sacred Scriptures,* edited by Kwok Pui-lan and Elisabeth Schüssler Fiorenza, 20–28. Concilium. Maryknoll, N.Y.: Orbis Books, 1998.

———. "From Storytelling to Written Text: The Loss of Early Christian Women's Voices." *Biblical Theology Bulletin* 26 (1996): 71–78.

———. "Gospel of Mark." In *Searching the Scriptures.* Vol. 2, *A Feminist Commentary,* edited by Elisabeth Schüssler Fiorenza, 470–509. New York: Crossroad, 1994.

———. *Markan Public Debate: Literary Technique, Concentric Structure, and Theology in Mark 2.1–3.6.* Chico, Calif.: Scholars Press, 1980.

———. "Mark as Interwoven Tapestry: Forecasts and Echoes for a Listening Audience." *Catholic Biblical Quarterly* 53 (1991): 221–36.

———. "Oral Methods of Structuring Narrative in Mark." *Interpretation* 43 (1990): 32–44.

———. "Women in the Synoptic Gospels: Seen But Not Heard?" *Biblical Theology Bulletin* 27, no. 2 (1997): 53–60.

Dibelius, Martin. *From Tradition to Gospel.* New York: Charles Scribner's Sons, 1934.

Donahue, John R. *Are You the Christ? The Trial Narrative in the Gospel of Mark.* Society of Biblical Literature Dissertation Series 10. Missoula, Mont. Scholars Press, 1973.

———. "Windows and Mirrors: The Setting of Mark's Gospel." *Catholic Biblical Quarterly* 57, no. 1 (1995): 1–26.

Donovan, Josephine. *Feminist Theory: The Intellectual Tradition of American Feminism.* New York: Ungar, 1985.

Dunning, James B. "Rite of Christian Initiation of Adults: Model of Adult Growth." *Worship* 53, no. 2 (1979): 142–56.

Dwyer, Timothy. *The Motif of Wonder in the Gospel of Mark.* Sheffield: Sheffield Academic Press, 1996.

Edwards, Denis. *Jesus the Wisdom of God: An Ecological Theology.* Maryknoll, N.Y.: Orbis Books, 1995.

Edwards, J. R. "Markan Sandwiches." *Novum Testamentum* 31 (1989): 193–216.

Erikson, Erik H. *Childhood and Society.* 35th Anniversary Edition. New York: W. W. Norton, 1985.

Eugene,Toinette. "Two Heads Are Better Than One," *Daughters of Sarah* (summer 1993): 1, 6–11.

Eusebius. *Ecclesiastical History.* Loeb Classical Library. London: Heinemann, 1926–32.

Fander, Monika. *Die Stellung der Frau im Markusevangelium: Unter besonderer Berücksichtigung kultur- und religion geschichtlicher Hintergrunde.* Altenberge: Telos Verlag, 1990.

Fetterley, Judith. *The Resisting Reader: A Feminist Approach to American Fiction.* Bloomington: Indiana University Press, 1978.

Fish, Stanley. *Is There a Text in This Class? The Authority of Interpretive Communities.* Cambridge, Mass.: Harvard University Press, 1980.

Fitzmyer, Joseph. "Priority of Mark and the 'Q' Source in Luke." In *To Advance the Gospel*, 3–40. New York: Crossroad, 1981.

Fowler, James W. *Becoming Adult, Becoming Christian.* San Francisco: Harper & Row, 1984.

———. *Stages of Faith: The Psychology of Human Development and the Quest for Meaning.* San Francisco: Harper & Row, 1981.

Fowler, Robert M. *Let the Reader Understand: Reader-Response Criticism and the Gospel of Mark.* Minneapolis: Augsburg-Fortress, 1991.

———. *Loaves and Fishes: The Function of the Feeding Stories in the Gospel of Mark.* Chico, Calif.: Scholars Press, 1981.

———. "The Rhetoric of Direction and Indirection in the Gospel of Mark." In *Reader Perspectives on the New Testament*, edited by Edgar V. McKnight, 115–46. Semeia 48. Atlanta: Scholars Press, 1989.

Frend, W. H. *The Early Church.* Philadelphia: Fortress Press, 1982.

Fuller, Reginald H. *The Formation of the Resurrection Narratives.* New York: Macmillan, 1971.

Gadamer, Hans-Georg. *Truth and Method.* New York: Seabury Press, 1975.

Geertz, Clifford. *The Interpretation of Cultures.* New York: Basic Books, 1973.

Gerhert, Mary, and James G. Williams, eds. *Genre, Narrativity, and Theology.* Semeia 43. Atlanta: Scholars Press, 1988.

Goulder, M. D. "Mark XVI.1–8." *New Testament Studies* 24 (1978): 235–40.

Good, Deirdre. "Pistis Sophia." In *Searching the Scriptures.* Vol. 2, *A Feminist Commentary*, edited by Elisabeth Schüssler Fiorenza, 678–707. New York: Crossroad, 1994.

Grant, Jacquelyn. *White Women's Christ and Black Women's Jesus: Feminist Christology and Womanist Response.* American Academy of Religion Academy Series 64. Atlanta: Scholars Press, 1989.

Grassi, Joseph A. *The Hidden Heroes of the Gospels: Female Counterparts of Jesus.* Collegeville, Minn: Liturgical Press, 1989.

———. "The Secret Heroine of Mark's Drama." *Biblical Theology Bulletin* 18 (1988): 10–15.

Haskins, Susan. *Mary Magdalen: Myth and Metaphor.* New York: Riverhead Books, 1993.

Hayes, Diana L. *Hagar's Daughters: Womanist Ways of Being in the World.* New York: Paulist, 1995.

Hedrick, C. W. "The Role of 'Summary Statements' in the Composition of the Gospel of Mark," *Novum Testamentum* 26 (1984): 289–311.

hooks, bell. *Feminist Theory: From Margin to Center.* Boston: South End Press, 1984.

———. *Yearning, Race, Gender, and Cultural Politics*. Boston: South End Press, 1990.

Hopkins, Clark. *The Discovery of Dura-Europos*. Edited by Bernard Goldman. New Haven: Yale University Press, 1979.

Hultgren, Arland J. *Jesus and His Adversaries: The Form and Function of the Conflict Stories in the Synoptic Tradition*. Minneapolis: Augsburg Publishing House, 1979.

Iser, Wolfgang. *The Act of Reading*. Baltimore: Johns Hopkins University Press, 1978.

———. "The Reading Process: A Phenomenological Approach." In *Reader-Response Criticism: From Formalism to Post-Structuralism*, edited by Jane P. Tompkins, 50–69. Baltimore: Johns Hopkins University Press, 1980.

Isasi-Diaz, Ada Maria. *En La Lucha: A Hispanic Woman's Liberation Theology*. Minneapolis: Fortress Press, 1993.

Isasi-Diaz, Ada Maria, and Yolanda Tarango, SC. *Hispanic Women: Prophetic Voice in the Church*. San Francisco: Harper & Row, 1988.

Jardine, Alice A. *Gynesis: Configurations of Women and Modernity*. Ithaca, N.Y.: Cornell University Press, 1985.

Johnson, Elizabeth A. *She Who Is: The Mystery of God in Feminist Theological Discourse*. New York: Crossroad, 1992.

Juel, Donald H. *Mark*. Augsburg Commentary on the New Testament. Minneapolis: Augsburg Fortress, 1990.

———. *A Master of Surprise: Mark Interpreted*. Minneapolis: Fortress Press, 1994.

———. *Messiah and Temple: The Trial of Jesus in the Gospel of Mark*. Society of Biblical Literature Dissertation Series 31. Missoula, Mont.: Scholars Press, 1977.

———. *Messianic Exegesis: Christological Interpretation of the Old Testament in Early Christianity*. Philadelphia: Fortress Press, 1988.

Karris, Robert J. *Luke, Artist and Theologian: Luke's Passion Account As Literature*. Mahwah, N.J.: Paulist Press, 1985.

Kealy, Sean P., CSSp. *Mark's Gospel: A History of Its Interpretation*. Ramsey, N.J.: Paulist Press, 1982.

Keifert, Patrick R. "Meaning and Reference: The Interpretation of Verisimilitude and the Gospel of Mark." Th.D. diss., University of Chicago, 1982.

———. "Mind Reader and Maestro: Models for Understanding Biblical Interpreters." In *A Guide to Contemporary Hermeneutics: Major Trends in Biblical Interpretation*, edited by Donald K. McKim, 220–38. Grand Rapids, Mich.: Eerdmans, 1986.

Kelber, Werner H. *The Oral and the Written Gospel*. Philadelphia: Fortress Press, 1983.

Kelber, Werner H., ed. *The Passion in Mark: Studies in Mark 14–16*. Philadelphia: Fortress Press, 1976.

Kelsey, David H. *The Uses of Scripture in Recent Theology.* Philadelphia: Fortress Press, 1975.

Kennedy, George A. *New Testament Interpretation Through Rhetorical Criticism.* Chapel Hill: University of North Carolina Press, 1984.

Kermode, Frank. *The Genesis of Secrecy: On the Interpretation of Narrative.* Cambridge, Mass.: Harvard University Press, 1979.

King, Karen L. "Canonization and Marginalization: Mary of Magdala." In *Women's Sacred Scriptures,* edited by Kwok Pui-lan and Elisabeth Schüssler Fiorenza, 29–36. Concilium 1998/3. Maryknoll, N.Y.: Orbis Books, 1998.

———. "The Gospel of Mary Magdalene." In *Searching the Scriptures.* Vol. 2, *A Feminist Commentary,* edited by Elisabeth Schüssler Fiorenza, 601–34. New York: Crossroad, 1994.

King, Ursala, ed. *Feminist Theology from the Third World: A Reader.* Maryknoll, N.Y.: Orbis Books, 1994.

Koester, Helmut. *Introduction to the New Testament.* Vol. 1, *History, Culture, and Religion of the Hellenistic Age.* New York: Walter de Gruyter, 1982.

———. *Introduction to the New Testament.* Vol. 2, *History and Literature of Early Christianity.* New York: Walter de Gruyter, 1982.

Kort, Wesley A. *Story, Text, and Scripture: Literary Interests in Biblical Narratives.* University Park: Pennsylvania State University Press, 1988.

Kristeva, Julia. *Desire in Language: A Semiotic Approach to Literature and Art.* Edited by Leon S. Roudiez. Translated by Thomas Gora, Alice Jardine, and Leon S. Roudiez. New York: Columbia University Press, 1980.

Kümmel, Werner Georg. *Introduction to the New Testament.* Translated by Howard Clark Kee. Nashville: Abingdon Press, 1986.

Kwok Pui-lan. "Racism and Ethnocentricism in Feminist Biblical Interpretation." In *Searching the Scriptures.* Vol. 1, *A Feminist Introduction,* edited by Elisabeth Schüssler Fiorenza, 101–16. New York: Crossroad, 1993.

Lategan, Bernard C., and Willem S. Vorster. *Text and Reality: Aspects of Reference in Biblical Texts.* Philadelphia: Fortress Press, 1985.

Lincoln, Andrew T. "The Promise and Failure, Mark 16.7-8." *Journal of Biblical Literature* 108, no. 2 (1989): 283–300.

Lindemann, Andreas. "Die Osterbotschaft des Markus: Zur Theologische Interpretation von Mark 16.1-8." *New Testament Studies* 26 (1980): 248–317.

Loder, James E. *The Transforming Moment: Understanding Convictional Experiences.* San Francisco: Harper & Row, 1981.

Longinus. *On the Sublime.* Translated by James A. Arieti and John M. Crossett. New York: Edwin Mellon Press, 1985.

Lord, Alfred B. *The Singer of Tales.* Cambridge, Mass.: Harvard University Press, 1960.

MacDonald, Dennis Ronald. *The Legend and the Apostle: The Battle for Paul in Story and Canon.* Philadelphia: Westminster Press, 1983.

Mack, Burton. *A Myth of Innocence: Mark and Christian Origins.* Philadelphia: Fortress Press, 1998.

————. *Rhetoric and the New Testament.* Philadelphia: Fortress Press, 1990.

Magness, J. Lee. *Sense and Absence: Structure and Suspension in the Ending of Mark's Gospel.* Atlanta: Scholars Press, 1986.

Malbon, Elizabeth Struthers. "Echoes and Foreshadowings in Mark 4–8: Reading and Rereading." *Journal of Biblical Literature* 112, no. 2 (1993): 211–30.

————. "Fallible Followers: Women and Men in the Gospel of Mark." In *The Bible and Feminist Hermeneutics,* edited by Mary Ann Tolbert, 29–48. Semeia 28. Chico, Calif.: Scholars Press, 1983.

————. *In the Company of Jesus: Characters in Mark's Gospel.* Louisville: Westminster John Knox Press, 2000.

————. "The Jewish Leaders in the Gospel of Mark: A Literary Study of Marcan Characterization." *Journal of Biblical Literature* 108, no. 2 (1989): 259–81.

————. *Narrative Space and Mythic Meaning in Mark.* San Francisco: Harper & Row, 1986.

Matera, Frank J. *The Kingship of Jesus: Composition and Theology in Mark 15.* Society of Biblical Literature Dissertation Series 66. Chico, Calif.: Scholars Press, 1982.

Matheson, Susan B. *Dura Europos.* New Haven: Yale University Art Gallery, 1982.

Marjanen, Antti. *The Woman Jesus Loved: Mary Magdalene in the Nag Hammadi Library and Related Documents.* Nag Hammadi and Manichaean Studies. New York: E. J. Brill, 1996.

————. *Passion Narratives and Gospel Theologies: Interpreting the Synoptics Through Their Passion Stories.* Mahwah, N.J.: Paulist Press, 1986.

Marshall, Christopher D. *Faith as a Theme in Mark's Narrative.* Cambridge: Cambridge University Press, 1989.

Marxsen, Willi. *Mark the Evangelist: Studies in the Redaction History of the Gospel.* Translated by James Boyce, Donald Juel, William Poehlmann with Roy A. Harrisville. New York: Abingdon, 1969.

McKnight, Edgar V., ed. *Reader Perspectives on the New Testament.* Semeia 48. Atlanta: Scholars Press, 1989.

Meier, John P. "The Brothers and Sisters of Jesus in Ecumenical Perspective." *Catholic Biblical Quarterly* 54 (1992): 1–28.

Metzger, Bruce M. *A Textual Commentary on the Greek New Testament: A Companion Volume to the United Bible Societies' Greek New Testament.* London: United Bible Societies, 1971.

————. *The Text of the New Testament: Its Transmission, Corruption, a Restoration.* 2nd ed. New York: Oxford University Press, 1969.

Meye, Robert P. *Jesus and the Twelve: Discipleship and Revelation in Mark's Gospel.* Grand Rapids, Mich.: Eerdmans, 1968.

Meyer, Marvin W. "Making Mary Male: The Categories 'Male' and 'Female' in the Gospel of Thomas." *New Testament Studies* 31 (1985): 554–70.

————. "The Youth in the Gospel of Secret Mark." In *The Apocryphal Jesus and*

Christian Origins, edited by Ron Cameron. Semeia 49. Atlanta: Scholars Press, 1990.

Mirecki, Paul Allan. "Mark 16:9–20: Composition, Tradition and Redaction." Th.D. diss., Harvard Divinity School, 1986. Ann Arbor: University Microfilms International Dissertation Information Services, 1986.

Morgan, Donn F. *Between Text and Community: The Writings in Canonical Interpretation*. Minneapolis: Fortress Press, 1990.

Moule, C. F. D. "St. Mark XVI.8 Once More." *New Testament Studies* 2 (1955): 58–59.

Munroe, Winsome. "Women Disciples in Mark." *Catholic Biblical Quarterly* 44, no. 2 (1982): 225–41.

Myers, Ched. *Binding the Strong Man: A Political Reading of Mark's Story of Jesus*. Maryknoll, N.Y.: Orbis Books, 1988.

Nag Hammadi Library in English. Edited by James M. Robinson. San Francisco: Harper & Row, 1978.

Newsom, Carol A., and Sharon Ringe, eds. *The Women's Bible Commentary*. Louisville: Westminster John Knox Press, 1992.

New Oxford Annotated Bible with the Apocryhpal/Deuterocanonical Books. New Revised Standard Version. Edited by Bruce M. Metzger and Roland E. Murphy. New York: Oxford University Press, 1991.

Novum Testamentum Graece. Edited by Eberhard Nestle, Erwin Nestle, Kurt Aland and others. 26th ed. Stuttgart: Deutsche Bibelgesellschaft, 1979.

O'Collins, Gerald. "Fearful Silence of the Women (Mark 16.8c)." *Gregorianum* 69 (1988): 489–503.

———. "Mary Magdalene as a Major Witness to Jesus' Resurrection." *Theological Studies* 48 (1987): 631–46.

Pagels, Elaine. *The Gnostic Gospels*. New York: Vantage Books, 1981.

Palmer, Richard E. *Hermeneutics*. Evanston: Northwestern University Press, 1969.

Parks, Sharon. *The Critical Years: The Young Adult Search for a Faith to Live By*. San Francisco: Harper & Row, 1986.

Perkins, Ann. *The Art of Dura-Europos*. Oxford: Oxford at the Clarendon Press, 1973.

Perkins, Pheme. "The Gospel of Thomas." In *Searching the Scriptures*. Vol. 2, *A Feminist Commentary*, edited by Elisabeth Schüssler Fiorenza, 535–60. New York: Crossroad, 1994.

Perkinson, Jim. "A Canaanitic Word in the Logos of Christ; or The Difference the Syro-Phoenician Woman Makes to Jesus." In *Postcolonialism and Scripture Reading*, 61-85. Semeia 75. Atlanta: Scholars Press, 1996.

Perrin, Norman. *The Resurrection According to Matthew, Mark, and Luke*. Philadelphia: Fortress Press, 1977.

Petersen, Norman R. *Literary Criticism for New Testament Critics*. Philadelphia: Fortress Press, 1978.

————. "Point of View in Mark's Narrative." In *Rhetoric, Eschatology, and Ethics in the New Testament,* edited by William A. Beardslee, 97–121. Semeia 12. Missoula, Mont.: Scholars Press, 1978.

————. "When Is the End Not the End? Literary Reflections on the Ending of Mark's Narrative." *Interpretation* 34 (1980): 151–66.

Phillips, Gary A. *Poststructural Criticism and the Bible: Text, History, Discourse.* Semeia 51. Atlanta: Scholars Press, 1990.

Plaskow, Judith. *Standing Again at Sinai: Judaism from a Feminist Perspective.* San Francisco: HarperSanFrancisco, 1990.

Poland, Lynn M. *Literary Criticism and Biblical Hermeneutics: A Critique of Formalist Approaches.* Chico, Calif.: Scholars Press, 1985.

Pomeroy, Sarah B. *Goddesses, Whores, Wives, and Slaves: Women in Classical Antiquity.* New York: Schocken Books, 1975.

Powell, Mark Alan. *What Is Narrative Criticism?* Minneapolis: Fortress Press, 1990.

Price, Robert. *The Widow Traditions in Luke-Acts: A Feminist Critical Study.* Society of Biblical Literature Dissertation Series 155. Atlanta: Scholars Press, 1997.

Rhoads, David, and Donald Michie. *Mark As Story: An Introduction to the Narrative of the Gospels.* Philadelphia: Fortress Press, 1982.

Ricci, Carla. *Mary Magdalene and Many Others: Women Who Followed Jesus.* Translated by Paul Burns. Minneapolis: Fortress Press, 1994.

Ricoeur, Paul. *Essays on Biblical Interpretation.* Edited by Lewis S. Mudge. Philadelphia: Fortress Press, 1980.

————. *Freud and Philosophy: An Essay on Interpretation.* Translated by Denis Savage. New Haven: Yale University Press, 1970.

————. *Interpretation Theory: Discourse and the Surplus of Meaning.* Fort Worth: Texas Christian University Press, 1976.

————. *The Rule of Metaphor: Multidisciplinary Studies of the Creation of Meaning in Language.* Translated by Robert Czerny with Kathleen McLaughlin and John Costello, S.J. Toronto: University of Toronto Press, 1977.

Ringe, Sharon H. *Wisdom's Friends: Community and Christology in the Fourth Gospel.* Louisville: Westminster John Knox Press, 1999.

Rizzuto, Ana-Maria. *The Birth of the Living God: A Psychoanalytic Study.* Chicago: University of Chicago Press, 1979.

Robbins, Vernon K. *Jesus the Teacher: A Socio-Rhetorical Interpretation of Mark.* Philadelphia: Fortress Press, 1984.

Rohrbaugh, Richard L. "The Social Location of the Markan Audience." *Biblical Theology Bulletin* 23, no. 3 (1993): 114–27.

Roman Missal: Lectionary for Mass Book of Gospels, New American Bible translation. New York: Catholic Book Publishing Company, 1984.

Ross, Mary Ellen. "Illusion and Reality in Freud and Winnicott: Toward a New Psychoanalytical Interpretation of Religion." *Soundings* 73 (1990): 465–79.

Rostovtzeff, M. *Dura-Europos and Its Art*. Oxford: Oxford at the Clarendon Press, 1938.

Rowland, Christopher, and Mark Corner. *Liberating Exegesis: The Challenge of Liberation Theology to Biblical Studies*. Louisville: Westminster/John Knox Press, 1989.

Ruether, Rosemary Radford. *Sexism and God-Talk: Toward a Feminist Theology*. Boston: Beacon Press, 1983.

Ryan, Rosalie. "Women from Galilee and Discipleship in Luke." *Biblical Theology Bulletin* 15 (1985): 56–59.

Schenke, Hans-Martin. "The Function and Background of the Beloved Disciple in the Gospel of John." In *Nag Hammadi Gnosticism and Early Christianity*, edited by Charles W. Hedrick and Robert Hodgson, Jr., 111–26. Peabody, Mass.: Hendrickson, 1986.

Schillebeeckx, Edward C. *Jesus: An Experiment in Christology*. New York: Seabury, 1978.

Schmidt, K. L. *Der Rahmen der Geschichte Jesu*. Berlin: Trowitzsch, 1919.

Schmithals, Walter. *Wunder und Glaube: Eine Auslange von Markus 4,35-6,6a*. Neukirchen-Vluyn: Neukirchener Verlag, 1970.

Schneiders, Sandra M., I.H.M. "Feminist Ideology and Biblical Hermeneutics." *Biblical Theology Bulletin* 19 (1989): 3–10.

———. *The Revelatory Text: Interpreting the New Testament as Sacred Scripture*. San Francisco: HarperSanFrancisco, 1991.

———. *With Oil in Their Lamps: Faith, Feminism, and the Future*. Mahwah, N.J.: Paulist Press, 2000.

———. *Women and the Word: The Gender of God in the New Testament and the Spirituality of Women*. New York: Paulist Press, 1986.

———. "Women in the Fourth Gospel and the Role of Women in the Contemporary Church." *Biblical Theology Bulletin* 12 (1982): 35–45.

———. *Written That You May Believe*. New York: Crossroad, 1999.

Schottroff, Luise. *Lydia's Impatient Daughters: A Feminist Social History of Early Christianity*. Translated by Barbara and Martin Rumscheidt. Louisville: Westminster John Knox Press, 1995.

———. "Maria Magdalena und die Frauen am Grabe Jesu." *Evangelische Theologie* 42 (1982): 3–25.

Schottroff, Luise, Silva Schroer, and Marie-Theres Wacker. *Feminist Interpretation: The Bible in Women's Perspective*. Translated by Martin and Barbara Rumscheidt. Minneapolis: Fortress Press, 1998.

Schüssler Fiorenza, Elisabeth. *Bread Not Stone: The Challenge of Feminist Biblical Interpretation*. Boston: Beacon Press, 1984.

———. "Breaking the Silence—Becoming Visible." In *Women Invisible in Church and Society*, edited by Elisabeth Schüssler Fiorenza and Mary Collins, 3–16. Concilium: Religion in the Eighties. Edinburgh: T & T Clark, 1985.

———. *But She Said: Feminist Practices of Biblical Interpretation*. Boston: Beacon Press, 1992.

———. "Changing the Paradigms." *Probe* 18, no. 5 (1990): 6–8. Reprinted from *Christian Century* 107, no. 25 (1990): 796–800.

———. *Discipleship of Equals: A Critical Feminist Ekklesia-logy of Liberation*. New York: Crossroad, 1993.

———. "The Ethics of Biblical Interpretation: Decentering Biblical Scholarship." *Journal of Biblical Literature* 107, no. 1 (1988): 3–17.

———. *In Memory of Her: A Feminist Theological Reconstruction of Christian Origins*. New York: Crossroad, 1985.

———. *Jesus: Miriam's Child, Sophia's Prophet: Critical Issues in Feminist Christology*. New York: Continuum, 1995.

———. "Martha and Mary, A Feminist Critical Interpretation for Liberation." *Religion & Intellectual Life* 3, no. 2 (1986): 21–35.

———. "The Politics of Otherness: Biblical Interpretation as a Critical Praxis of Liberation." In *Expanding the View: Gustavo Gutiérrez and the Future of Liberation Theology*, edited by Marc H. Ellis and Otto Jadura, 315–18. Maryknoll, N.Y.: Orbis Books, 1988.

———. "The 'Quilting' of Women's History: Phoebe of Cenchreae." *In Embodied Love: Sensuality and Relationships as Feminist Values*, edited by Paula M. Cooey, Sharon A. Farmer, and Mary Ellen Ross, 35–50. San Francisco: Harper & Row, 1987.

———. *Sharing Her Word: Feminist Biblical Interpretation in Context*. Boston: Beacon Press, 1998.

———. "Text and Reality—Reality as Text: The Problem of a Feminist Historical and Social Reconstruction Based on Texts." *Studia Theologia* 43 (1989): 19–34.

———. "The Twelve." In *Women Priests: A Catholic Commentary on the Vatican Declaration*, edited by Leonard Swidler and Arlene Swidler, 114–22. Ramsey, N.J.: Paulist Press, 1977.

Schüssler Fiorenza, Francis. "The Crisis of Scriptural Authority, Interpretation and Reception." *Interpretation* 44, no. 4 (1990): 353–68.

Schweitzer, Albert. *The Quest of the Historical Jesus: A Critical Study of Its Progress from Reimarus to Wrede*. New York: Macmillan, 1968.

Scott, M. P. "Chiastic Structures: A Key to the Interpretation of Mark's Gospel." *Biblical Theology Bulletin* 15 (1985): 17–26.

Senior, Donald. "With Sword and Clubs." *Biblical Theology Bulletin* 17 (1987): 10–20.

Selvidge, Marla J. "'And Those Who Followed Feared' (Mark 10.32)." *Catholic Biblical Quarterly* 45 (1983): 396–400.

———. *Daughters of Jerusalem*. Kitchener: Herald Press, 1987.

———. *Women, Cult, and Miracle Recital: A Redactional Critical Investigation of Mark 5.24–34*. Lewisburg, Pa.: Bucknell University Press, 1990.

Setzer, Claudia. "Excellent Women: Female Witnesses to the Resurrection." *Journal of Biblical Literature* 116, no. 2 (1997): 259–72.

Sharing the Light of Faith: National Catechetical Directory for Catholics in the United States. Washington, DC: U.S. Catholic Conference, 1979.

Sobrino, Juan Luis. *The Historical Jesus of the Synoptics.* Translated by John Drury. Maryknoll, N.Y.: Orbis Books, 1985.

Stanton, Elizabeth Cady. *The Women's Bible,* Parts I, II. Reprint Edition. New York: Arno Press, 1972.

Stegemann, Ekkehard W. "Zur Rolle von Petrus, Jakobus und Johannes im Markusevangelium." *Theologische Zeitschrift* 42 (1986): 366–74.

Steinhauser, M. G. "Mk 10.46–52." *New Testament Studies* 32, no. 4 (1986): 583–95.

Stock, Augustine. "Chiastic Awareness and Education in Antiquity." *Biblical Theology Bulletin* 14 (1984): 223–27.

———. "Hinge Transitions in Mark's Gospel." *Biblical Theology Bulletin* 15 (1985): 27–31.

Swanson, Richard W. "Parable and Promises Not Kept." Th.D. diss., Luther Seminary, 1991.

Swartley, Willard M. "The Role of Women in Mark's Gospel: A Narrative Analysis." *Biblical Theology Bulletin* 27, no. 1 (1997): 16–22.

Talley, Thomas J. *The Origins of the Liturgical Year.* New York: Pueblo Publishing, 1986.

Tannehill, Robert C. "The Disciples in Mark: The Function of a Narrative Role." *Journal of Religion* 57, no. 4 (1977): 386–405.

———. "The Gospel of Mark as Narrative Christology." In *Perspectives on Mark's Gospel,* edited by Norman R. Petersen, 57–96. Semeia 16. Missoula, Mont.: Scholars Press, 1979.

———. *The Sword of His Mouth.* Philadelphia: Fortress Press, 1975.

Theissen, Gerd. *The Gospels in Context: Social and Political History in the Synoptic Tradition.* Philadelphia: Fortress Press, 1991.

———. *Miracle Stories of the Early Christian Tradition.* Philadelphia: Fortress Press, 1983

———. *Sociology of Early Palestinian Christianity.* Philadelphia: Fortress Press, 1978.

Thiselton, Anthony C. *The Two Horizons.* Grand Rapids, Mich.: Eerdmans, 1980.

Thistlethwaite, Susan Brooks. *Sex, Race, and God: Christian Feminism in Black and White.* New York: Crossroad, 1989.

Tolbert, Mary Ann. "Defining the Problem: The Bible and Feminist Hermeneutics." In *The Bible and Feminist Hermeneutics,* edited by Mary Ann Tolbert, 113–26. Semeia 28. Chico, Calif.: Scholars Press, 1983.

———. "Protestant Feminists and the Bible: On the Horns of a Dilemma." In *The Pleasure of Her Text,* edited by Mary Ann Tolbert, 5–25. Philadelphia: Trinity Press International, 1991.

————. *Sowing the Gospel: Mark's World in Literary-Historical Perspective*. Minneapolis: Fortress Press, 1989.

Tompkins, Jane P. "The Reader in History: The Changing Shape of Literary Response." In *Reader-Response Criticism: From Formalism to Post-Structuralism*, edited by Jane P. Tompkins, 201–32. Baltimore: Johns Hopkins University Press, 1980.

Tracy, David. *Plurality and Ambiguity: Hermeneutics, Religion, Hope*. San Francisco: Harper & Row, 1987.

Tracy, David, and Robert M. Grant. *A Short History of the Interpretation of the Bible*. Philadelphia: Fortress Press, 1984.

Trible, Phyllis. *God and the Rhetoric of Sexuality*. Overtures to Biblical Theology 2. Philadelphia: Fortress Press, 1978.

————. *Texts of Terror: Literary-Feminist Readings of Biblical Narratives*. Overtures to Biblical Theology 13. Philadelphia: Fortress Press, 1984.

Ulanov, Ann Belford. *Finding Space: Winnicott, God, and Psychic Reality*. Louisville: Westminster John Knox Press, 2001.

Wainwright, Elaine M. *Shall We Look for Another? A Feminist Rereading of the Matthean Jesus*. Maryknoll, N.Y.: Orbis Books, 1998

————. *Towards a Feminist Critical Reading of the Gospel According to Matthew*. Berlin: Walter de Gruyter, 1991.

Weeden, Theodore J. *Mark—Traditions in Conflict*. Philadelphia: Fortress Press, 1971.

West, Gerald, and Musa W. Dube, eds. *Reading With: An Exploration of the Interface Between Critical and Ordinary Readings of the Bible, African Overtures*. Semeia 73. Atlanta: Scholars Press, 1996.

Wilder, Amos N. *The Bible and the Literary Critic*. Minneapolis: Fortress Press, 1991.

————. *Early Christian Rhetoric*. Cambridge, Mass.: Harvard University Press, 1971.

Williams, James G. *Gospel Against Parable: Mark's Language of Mystery*. Decatur, Ill.: Almond Press, 1985.

Index of Ancient Sources

Index of Names

150